practical CLASSICS
& Car Restorer
ON
SUNBEAM RAPIER
RESTORATION

Reprinted from
Practical Classics magazine

ISBN 1 870642 120

Published by
PPG Publishing Ltd. with the permission of *Practical Classics*

practical CLASSICS

Distributed by:

Brooklands Book Distribution Ltd.,
Holmerise, Seven Hills Road,
Cobham, Surrey KT11 1ES,
England.   Tel: 09326 5051

Motorbooks International,
Osceola,
Wisconsin 54020 U.S.A.
Tel: 715 294 3345

Introduction

We acquired KHG 474 late in 1980, and first wrote about it in our May 1981 issue – and at the time of writing (February 1988) the car is still with us! During the seven years in between it's undergone an extensive rebuild, contested two special-stage Coronation Rallies, and been subjected to almost continuous everyday use including commuting in the hands of various staff members.

All this has proved to us what thoroughly practical and reliable transport the Minx-based Rootes saloons represent – cheap to buy (even now a good Rapier can be found for under £1,000, and a Minx for little more than half that sum), blessed with a good club back-up, and with a reasonable parts situation, the cars can be recommended to both the beginner in classic motoring or to the more experienced enthusiast who wants a characterful car at an affordable price. The Rapier can still be a successful competition car too and after contesting the Coronation Rally our respect for its handling qualities grew enormously (with a completely standard engine we weren't that far away from winning our class).

However, we expect that most of you reading these words will already own a Rootes saloon so won't need much convincing; if so, we hope that our experience, as recounted in these pages, will help you to maintain and improve your car more easily. Meanwhile, our own Series IIIA Rapier, rescued from a scrapman for £50, continues to provide yeoman service; although, as it was expected to be sold by the spring of 1988, perhaps in the hands of someone other than a *Practical Classics* staff member.

Paul Skilleter

RAPIER REVIVAL!

If you own a Rootes Rapier or its Minx or Gazelle cousin, you won't want to miss our new series on restoring this Sixties favourite.

Quite frankly, we bought our 1960 Sunbeam Rapier by accident — contributor Lindsay Porter spotted it at a local scrapyard and we decided it was worth forking out the necessary £50 to rescue it from the inevitable. Having bought it, we then weren't too sure what to do with it, because while the interior was unusually good the rest of the car certainly wasn't, and one has to consider the economics of rebuilding a 'cheap' car, where the finished result will be nowhere near valuable enough to cover the costs involved.

However, encouraged by the sheer enthusiasm of Rapier owners, and the fact that much of the car's body and mechanics are shared by other Rootes cars, we finally plumped for a full rebuild. And step number one was to discover just what we were up against, so the Rapier went up on axle stands and under we crawled armed with a lead-light and screwdriver. Our initial impression was that while the car had rust in all the usual places on the external panels (wing lips, sills, a few pimples at the bottoms of the doors, around the headlights and so on), structurally it seemed very sound.

The difficult bit is going to be the outer panels because, of course, there are no new ones to be found (and even if we did manage to conjure some up, we wouldn't use them

— as with most of our restorations, we're going to tackle the Rapier using resources available to the average enthusiast, and that won't generally include new Rapier panels!). However, David Parrot of the Sunbeam Rapier Owners Club, who has already given us much good advice, says that front wings are the same as Hillman Minxes of the same period — so, you've guessed it, we're going to investigate the condition of every *circa* 1960 Minx we can locate in our favourite scrapyards!

One thing is in our favour — our particular Rapier has obviously been looked after and so far as we can tell, has never been crashed and apart from some localised touching up, has never been resprayed. Add this to complete originality and an excellent set of seats and interior trim, and we think we have the ideal basis for what we hope will turn out to be a very nice car indeed. Well — stay with us for the next 8-12 months and you'll see if we're right!

The excellent interior of our Rapier was a major factor in favour of giving the car the full-rebuild treatment.

The engine bay was equally original and complete, but we will be stripping the engine to trace a persistent mis-fire.

> **NEXT MONTH**
> We carry out a pre-build examination

Rapier Restoration!

We discover what we're up against as we give our 1960 Sunbeam Rapier a searching examination — and start investigating the parts scene. Paul Skilleter continues the story.

If you're about to commence a full restoration, it's best that you know the worst before you begin — so before starting work, we jacked the Rapier up, placed it on axle stands, and looked very carefully at the vital bits of the underside. In fact this elementary precaution may very well prevent distress later, if you happen to have a car which turns out to be too far gone underneath, but you hadn't noticed and proceeded to put time and money into other areas first.

So we took up our trusty old battery lamp, an equally old screw-driver, and a clipboard on which to note down the worst, and got down to it. Rust in the outer panels was self-evident and didn't require too much detective work — all the usual places in wings, wheel arches and sills were effected, although bar a few blisters, the doors appear sound at this stage (the real truth will be revealed on removing the paint). But a previous, and rather cursory, look underneath had suggested that the main structure was surprisingly good for a 1960 car.

This belief was substantiated to a reasonable degree by our more detailed probings with the screw-driver, which failed to reveal serious rust in the integral chassis rails or spring mounting points. The only place where the car was worse than we thought was in a typical Rapier/Minx/Gazelle problem area — where the inner sill wall joins the front wheel arch.

Rust usually sets in at this point in a big way after the wheel arch itself corrodes through, allowing water and mud to enter the hollow sill and collect along its length, but especially

Rapier Restoration!

Rust damage to outer panels is usually all too obvious — this picture shows the ample amount of corrosion all round the rear wheel arch.

View looking forward to front spring anchorage, showing drilled cross-member and (right) non-existent closing plate to sill which has rusted away.

Bottom of rear wing behind wheel is double skinned and trapped moisture leads to rust; rear spring mounting is another (and rather more important) danger spot though our Rapier was sound here.

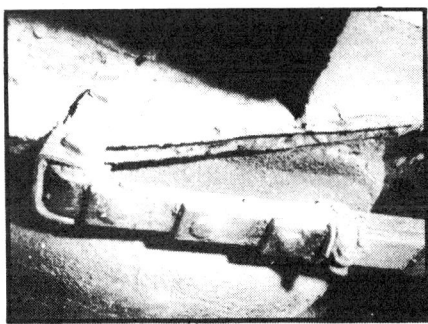

Another view of the rear spring mounting, and of the chassis box member — as can be seen it runs very close to the petrol tank and often corrodes at this point.

at the front. The inner wall of the sill then begins to rot here, followed by the footwell — and this is what has happened to our Rapier. The sills are also holed at their rear ends, in front of the rear wheels, but this had been immediately visible from the outset.

There are very unlikely to be any repair sections (or underside panels of any description) available from commercial sources, so we shall be making up new parts for the inner sills and floor as we go along — and as no particularly difficult shapes appear to be involved, this should cause no problems. The real difficulty with the bodywork is, of course, going to occur when it comes to repairing the outer panels, as we can hardly expect to find new Rapier wings on the shelf anywhere. But as we mentioned last month, David Parrot of the Sunbeam Rapier Owners Club advises that the Rapier's front wings are the same as the Minx of equivalent vintage, and there may thus be more of a chance of locating these (new or good second-hand) than the finned rears which are unique to the Rapier.

However, it might be that parts of the Minx rear wing may also be the same as the Rapier's, up to the waistline anyway — given that the Minx item would be shorter, the Hillman being a four-door car as opposed to the Sunbeam which is a two-door vehicle. It is for this same reason that you can't use Minx front doors on the Rapier, as they are smaller than the Sunbeam's. David Parrott says that the convertible Minxes and Gazelles share the Rapier doors — but we suspect that the rarity of these cars means that owners look out for good scrap Rapier doors for their cars, rather than the other way about! While we haven't investigated the situation fully, it seems that the only new panels you can get from Talbot these days are outer sills, which is hardly surprising. We will, however, be bringing you a list of whatever new panels or proprietory repair sections are generally available for Rapiers (and Minxes), from whatever source,

On the mechanical front, things are much better, and it seems that you can get virtually everything to rebuild the engine, transmission and brakes of a Rapier. We'll soon be finding out, anyway! One thing we've got to tackle, incidentally, is the non-functioning overdrive (this was an optional extra on the Rapier, and provides very relaxed cruising; can't wait to get the car running!). Chrome bits are very scarce though, and it'll be a question of seeing what turns up and hunting through autojumble stalls and the like for things like the dummy front vent grilles (which rust right through), badges and so on.

Typical front-end rust spots on a Rapier — at top rear of front wing, and where it meets the door all the way down.

This looks as if it's going to be a tricky repair — rust holes in the inner wing all the way along the side of the engine bay; the other side is the same too; you can see the Managing Ed. probing for them in our heading picture.

Of course rust sets in all round the front wheel arch, and at bottom where the wing meets sill.

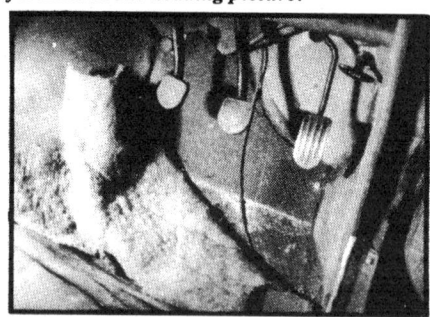

Signs of deterioration in the floor can also be detected by pulling up the carpet and the ample amounts of sound-deadening felt present in the footwell and poking with a screwdriver.

Neat — the Rapier's boot is hardly marked, and note the excellent condition of floor including where it joins the wheel arches, and the unrusted rear damper mountings at the back. Most cars have their good points, and this along with the interior is one of the Rapier's.

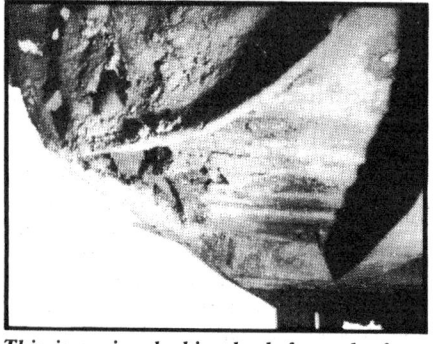

This is a view looking back from the front suspension. It shows that the inner sill has well and truly gone where it meets the wheel arch, as has the adjacent floor. Main integral chassis member right is completely sound, however.

Our first step on the spares trail was to join the Sunbeam Rapier Owners Club, which has a spares scheme which a member can join for a small extra donation — if you want to get an application form, write to David Parrot at 185 Milton Road, Cowplain, Hants PO8 8SF. Minx and Gazelle owners may find it helpful

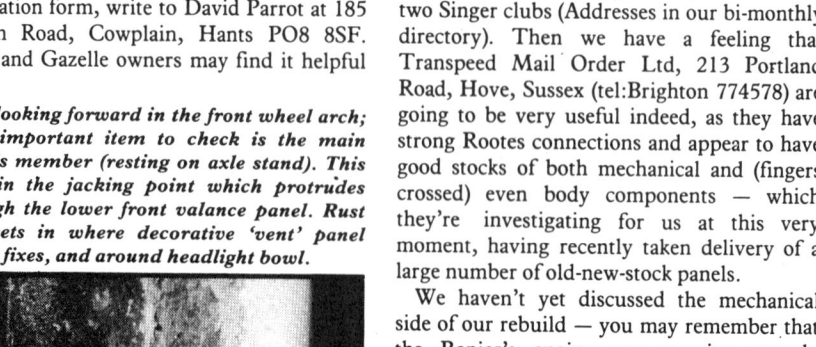

View looking forward in the front wheel arch; most important item to check is the main chassis member (resting on axle stand). This ends in the jacking point which protrudes through the lower front valance panel. Rust also sets in where decorative 'vent' panel ▼ *fixes, and around headlight bowl.*

to join the new Hillman Owners Club (66 St Georges Road, Durseley, Glos.) or one of the two Singer clubs (Addresses in our bi-monthly directory). Then we have a feeling that Transpeed Mail Order Ltd, 213 Portland Road, Hove, Sussex (tel:Brighton 774578) are going to be very useful indeed, as they have strong Rootes connections and appear to have good stocks of both mechanical and (fingers crossed) even body components — which they're investigating for us at this very moment, having recently taken delivery of a large number of old-new-stock panels.

We haven't yet discussed the mechanical side of our rebuild — you may remember that the Rapier's engine was running sweetly except for a misfire, and the aforementiopned (optional) overdrive wasn't working. Well, the engine will be stripped and rebuilt, with the same going for the suspension and brakes, all of which are basically similar to Hillman Minxes of the same age (so there's more encouragement for all Rootes owners!). In fact the first real steps in the rebuild will probably be yanking the engine out — and that's what we hope to talk about next month, together with more news on the parts front.

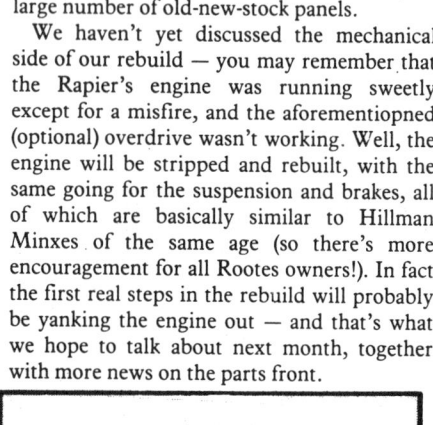

NEXT MONTH

Taking the engine out.

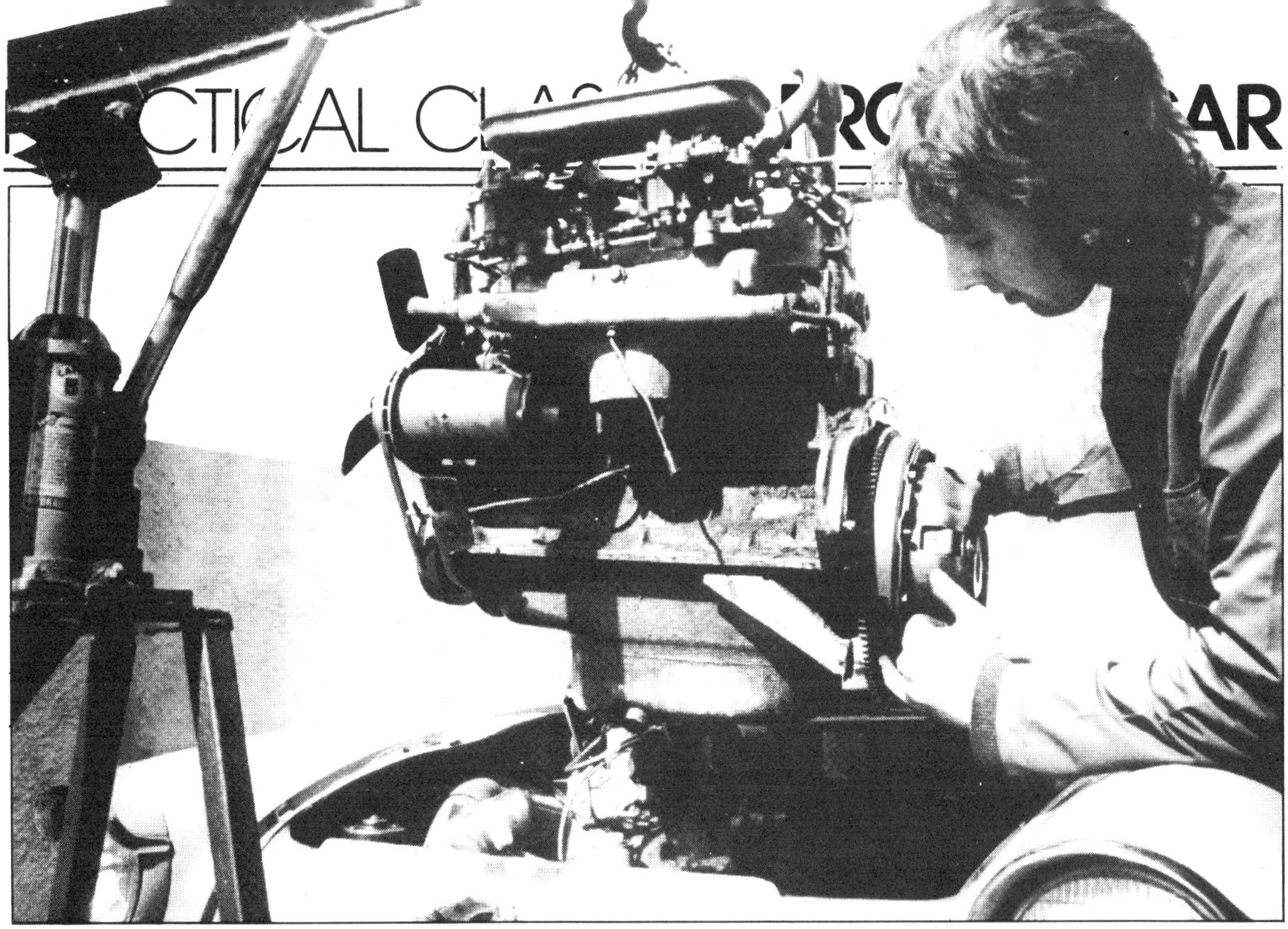

Rapier Restoration!

*Engine removal practices explained as we proceed
with the restoration of this classic sports saloon.
Paul Skilleter takes up the story.*

There's no way you can properly restore a car *and* leave the engine in — for a start you simply can't clean the engine bay properly, let alone repaint it, and indeed any attempt to paint the underbonnet areas without doing so will probably end up as a disastrous mess. In any case, with most engines you can't get a proper look at the condition of the main bearings without taking the unit out, and we certainly wanted to take that precaution with our 1960 car even though no bearing noise had been evident before taking the car off the road.

You can start by removing the bonnet — four ½-ins AF bolts to undo and then lift clear; scribing round bolts first will help when refitting the bonnet later.

If you haven't removed an engine before, it's certainly not something to be intimidated by, and the procedure we followed with the Rapier is much the same for any car of the period — including its close relatives the Minx, Gazelle and Alpine sports car (whose engine it shared from September 1959, when in Series III form the Rapier adopted the Alpine's 9.2:1 c.r. alloy head). The best overall advice we can give is, work methodically and don't hurry.

The main stages are followed in the pictures, but there are some additional points to mention. First, remove the battery — it's in the way, and it's not very safe to disconnect the electrics when current is running through them, especially as you'll be undoing petrol

9

Rapier Restoration!

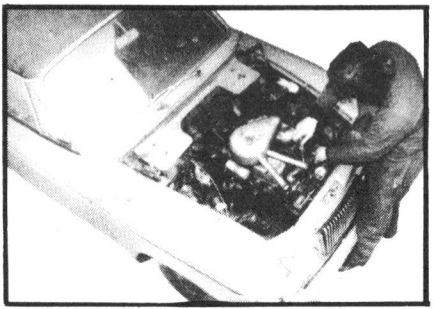

Everything is easier to see with the bonnet away; having drained the coolant, Terry is disconnecting top and bottom hoses from the radiator.

Four ½-ins AF bolts hold the radiator in place; with these undone the radiator can be lifted out.

Coil comes away with the air cleaner and its bracket, this being attached to the cylinder head; another bracket locates the air cleaner at the front, bolted to the thermostat housing.

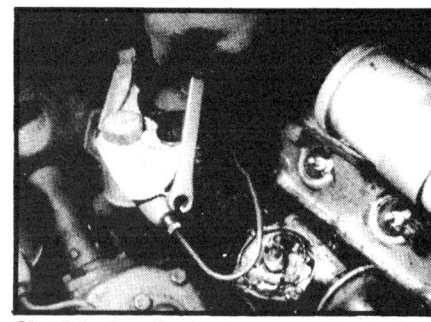

Clutch hydraulic pipe is removed from clutch master cyl. reservoir — note useful spanner for this type of job. Polythene under reservoir cap creates airlock and saves fluid leaking out. Clutch slave cylinder is removed entirely, otherwise it may foul bulkhead.

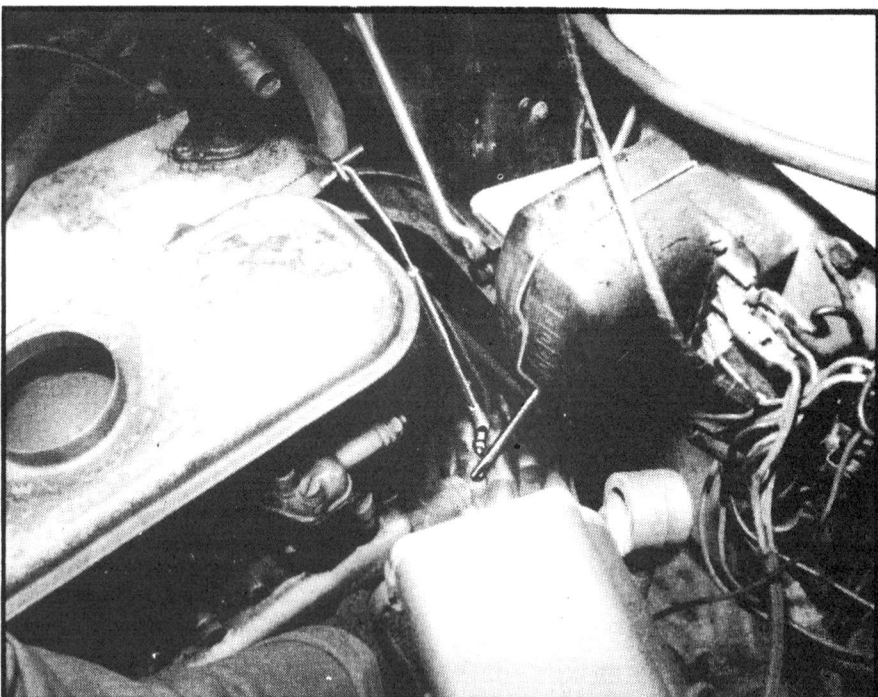

Throttle linkage is detached by undoing a small bolt underneath voltage regulator, and undoing the two 7/16-ins bolts which secure the bulkhead-mounted bracket.

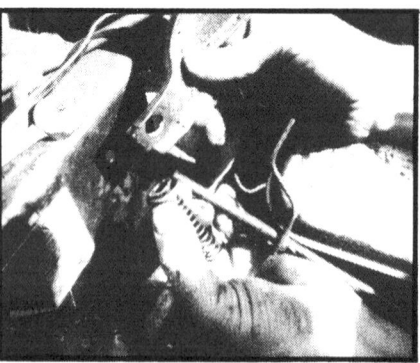

The bracket supports the linkage where it runs to the carbs, via a spring clip. Don't lose the bits and pieces which are now loose. Choke cable must also be detached — clamp and screw on spindle.

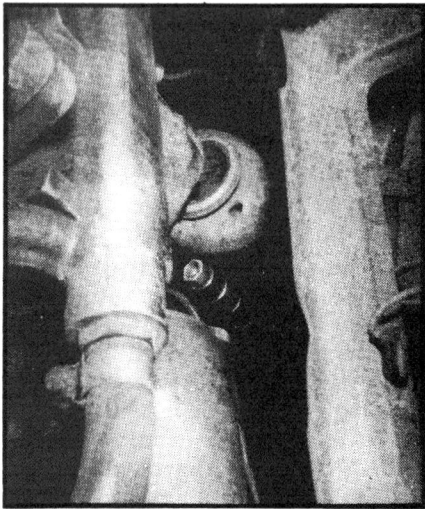

Removing the two 9/16-ins brass nuts holding exhaust downpipe to manifold can be tricky — it is best tackled by laying under thr car and using a socket on the end of a double extension.

lines as well. On the subject of electrics, don't forget to disconnect high and low tension leads from the coil before lifting it away with the air cleaner to which it is fixed. Remove the distributor cap complete with leads (mark them if it's not obvious which plug each goes to), and remove the rotor arm to prevent accidental damage to it. The rev. counter drive must be disconnected from the distributor base too.

The wiring from dynamo and starter should be disconnected, the latter from the solenoid which is easier. The starter can be left in place, incidentally, until the engine has been seperated from the bell-housing later on, when the job becomes simpler. The nearside Windtone horn is best removed (two 7/16-ins bolts) because it gets in the way, but you can leave the other one in place.

Separating the exhaust downpipe from the manifold can cause frayed tempers. The best way to approach this job is to jack the front of the car up, place it on axle stands, get underneath and use both extensions from your socket set to reach up past the starter to the 9/16-ins brass nuts securing pipe to manifold.

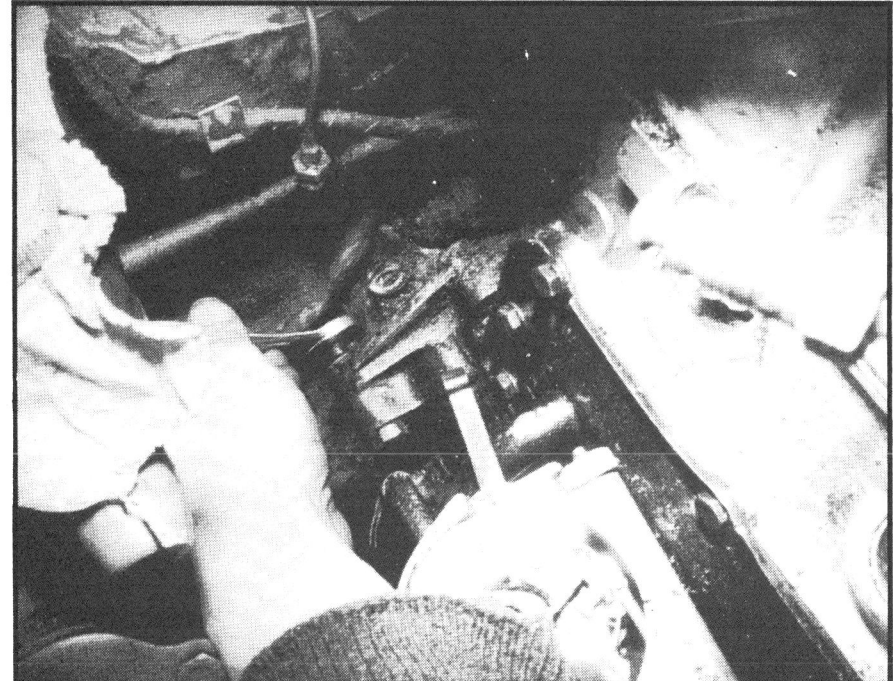

With all other connections severed too, the 9/16-ins bolts holding engine to bell-housing (and including the starter motor bolts) can be undone.

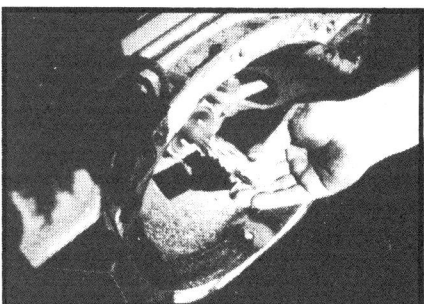

Gearbox splines should always be greased, to avoid rusting which, apart from anything else, will make refitting the engine extra difficult.

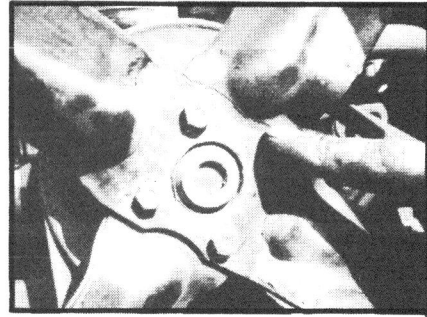

A quick glance at the engine revealed cracked fan blades, which if undiscovered could have broken and possibly wrecked the radiator.

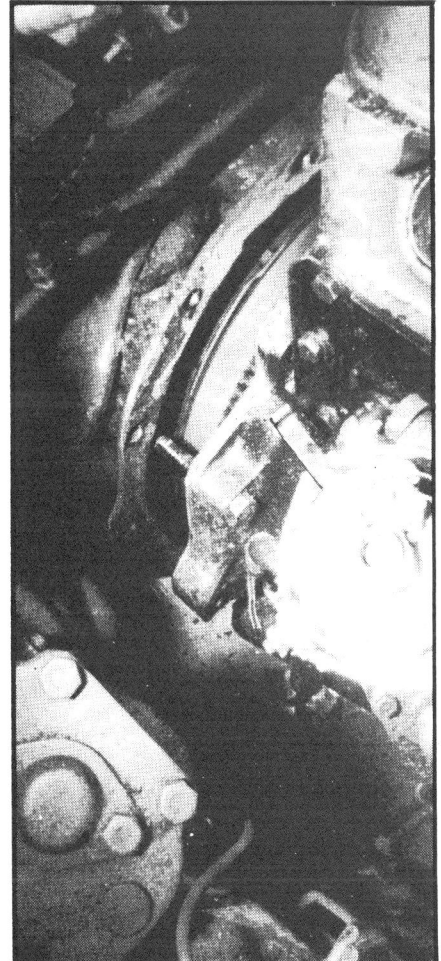

Engine should be inched forward until free of any dowel bolts and gearbox drive shaft splines, then upwards. Engine mounts, if they've been left attached to engine, can then be removed with ease.

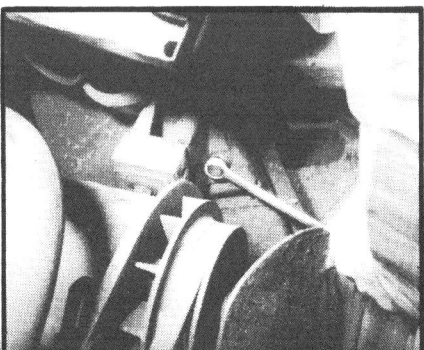

It can be easier to undo the engine mounting brackets at their base first, where they attach to the engine bay side (right of photo).

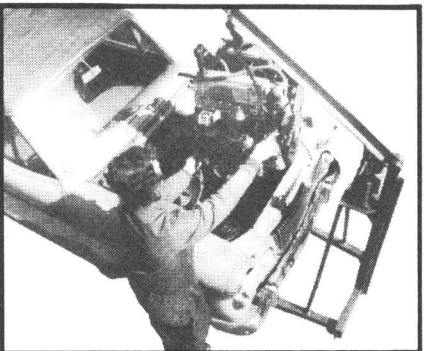

Up she comes! The Rapier's engine leaves its home, possibly for the first time.

You'll need more leverage than the speedbrace can supply, incidentally, so use the tommy bar then the ratchet.

Other points to note include disconnecting the fuel pipe from the filter bowl, the oil pressure gauge engine-to-bulkhead flexible pipe (you can leave the flexible section attached to the engine), and the earth lead when you tackle the nearside engine mounting

bracket. When you come to the bell housing area, there are four 7/16-ins bolts holding the clutch blanking cover (or dirt shield) in place — this should be allowed to drop down out of the way, from between crankcase and bell housing.

You can take the engine out complete with gearbox if you wish, but in view of the weight then involved, separating the two as we've done is probably the best method. We'll be talking about gearbox removal in the next issue. The gearbox should be supported on a trolley jack before you disconnect it from the engine, and afterwards secured in place. The engine is best lifted using the brackets which are (or were) provided by the manufacturer, diagonally at each end of the engine. If these are missing, sling adequately strong rope round each end of the engine, making sure it can't slip out of place. It is possible for a couple of people to manually lift the engine clear of the car, using this rope attached to a

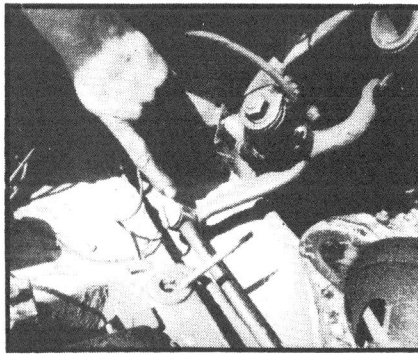

The typical Rootes steering arm connection — a taper fit, it is notoriously difficult to get at with the engine in place so we'll take this opportunity of making quite sure it's OK before the engine goes back in.

Rapier Restoration!

It's quite true, you can usually only give an engine bay a proper clean when the power unit's out. We've not yet decided whether to just do this, or strip the bulkhead for repainting entirely — it may depend on what bodywork repairs are required.

strong piece of timber, but we strongly recommend you hire a crane or hoist of the type we used — it really is much safer, and will only cost a few pounds for a weekend's use.

Removing the engine from the Rapier took only around three hours, so it is not a particularly big or difficult job.

As we said at the beginning, be methodical and in particular, make a final, detailed inspection to make sure that all connections between engine and car have indeed been severed before trying to lift the engine out. Bear in mind too that a certain amount of wriggling and persuading is often needed to separate the engine from the bell-housing, and it is important to maintain the correct angle so that the engine pulls easily off the drive shaft splines — gentle levering between crankcase and bell housing is permissable if stubborness is encountered, but don't overdo it or you'll break the aluminium bell housing. And when the engine is free, don't go merrily hoisting the engine out at a fast pace — take it slowly and keep checking that your aren't fouling an underbonnet component.

You should plan where you are going to put your engine before you start work — it may well influence where you position the car, particularly as it is not very safe to move an engine dangling from a crane, as you might create a pendulum effect. If you must do this, lower the engine so that it's just clear of the ground, so if the worst happens it's hardly got any distance to fall.

NEXT MONTH

Removing the gearbox and overdrive, and taking the cylinder head off the block.

Rapier Restoration!

Paul Skilleter details another stage in the restoration of our 1960 Series III Sunbeam Rapier — and finds that KHG 474's engine has had a lucky escape . . .

You may remember that when we rescued our basically very original Series III Rapier from the scrapman, the engine exhibited a persistent misfire which no amount of fiddling with plugs and points would cure. We talked about various possible causes for this, like bent valves or broken valve springs, but the one big clue was water loss from the cooling system — and it wasn't dripping onto the ground either. A sure sign of head gasket failure, we concluded.

Last month we covered the removal of the engine, so it was a simple job to confirm our diagnosis by removing the cylinder head from the block — a task which is followed in detail by the photographs and which applies in principle to all the Rootes cars with this basic engine (including Minx, Gazelle and Alpine).

We started by brushing the exterior of the unit down with paraffin and giving it a good general clean, which makes the work easier and more pleasant, and a little over an hour later the head was separated from the block.

We encountered no real problems and it was obvious that this engine hasn't been dismantled very many times before, as none of the nuts were rounded and nothing was missing. But as soon as the head was lifted, the

Rapier Restoration!

(Continued)

First task was to clean the removed engine with paraffin, after which the removal of ancilliaries like the advance/retard vacuum pipe shown here could begin.

Petrol feed pipe to the twin Zenith carburettors was taken off, and water hose to inlet manifold disconnected.

At the rear of the inlet manifold the water pipe to the block was also disconnected (gland nut).

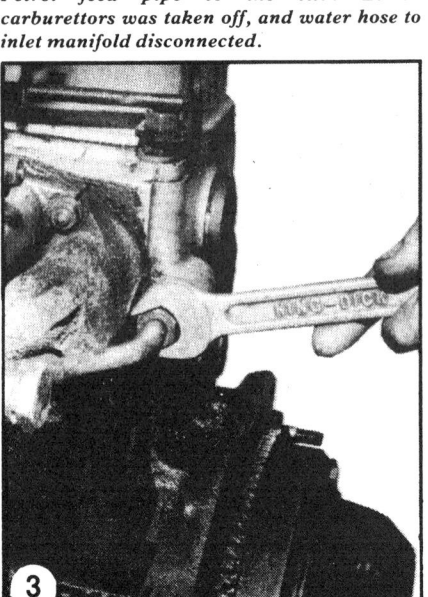

It was then a case of removing the nuts — plus the one long centre bolt — which secured the inlet manifold to block.

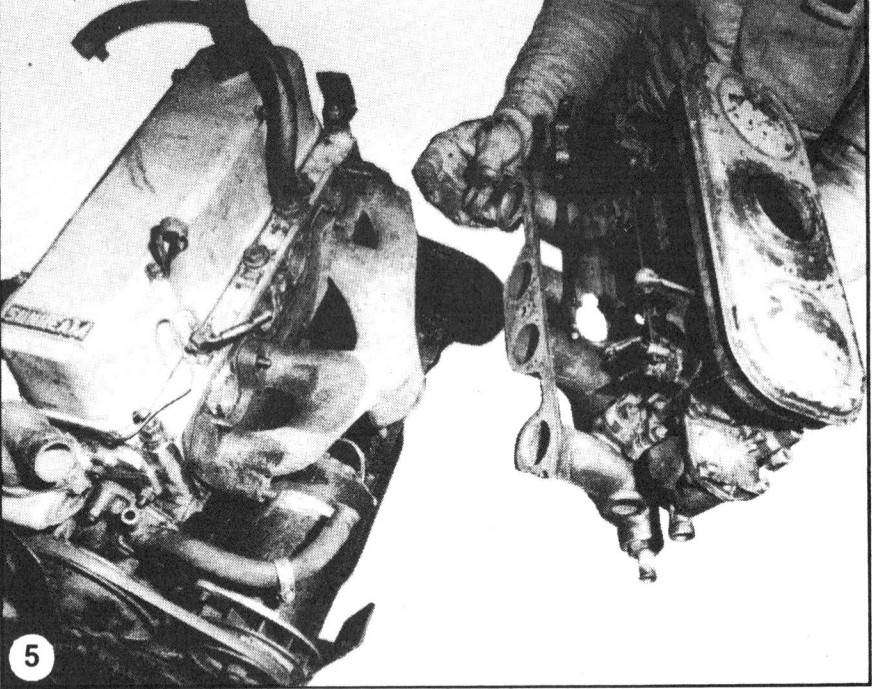

The inlet manifold complete with carbs was then lifted clear — don't lose inserts on outer induction ports. Exhaust manifold is easily removed as clamp securing its centre becomes accessible once the inlet manifold is out of the way.

reason why the poor old Rapier hadn't been very happy became obvious at once — just as we'd thought, coolant had indeed been entering the cylinders, and in considerable quantities.

In fact it was lucky that the engine hadn't been seriously damaged through hydraulic lock-up, caused by the incompressability of water which can result in bent con-rods and worse, such was the amount we found. Three out of the four cylinders contained congealed masses of anti-freeze and general gunge, and

some of the valves were actually rusty. Neither Terry or I had seen anything quite so bad before.

The cause? Almost certainly the failure of somebody to tighten the head down properly after replacing the head gasket — as simple as that. Otherwise the engine seems very well preserved, and scraping the piston crowns showed that the pistons and therefore bores are standard — and we doubt very much if the bottom end of the engine has ever been disturbed since it left the factory in 1960.

CONTINUED ON PAGE 20

6 The big aluminium rocker cover is taken off by undoing four nuts.

7 Terry lifts the rocker cover clear and we get a first look at some of the engine's internals; nothing unusual at this stage, except for some rather emulsified oil.

8 One cause of the misfire, the engine was suffering, could possibly have been a broken valve spring, but a quick check revealed that this wasn't the cause so far as our Rapier was concerned.

9 The rocker shaft was the next item tackled, commencing with the oil feed to the shaft.

10 When undoing the rocker shaft pedestal nuts it is best to loosen each one first, so that the valve springs push the shaft upwards gradually — otherwise it can jam.

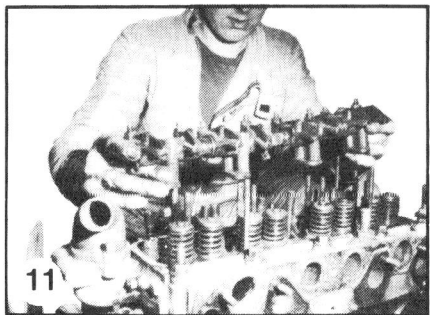

11 Terry lifts the rocker shaft clear of the head.

12 The shaft is actually split, the two halves being joined by the oil feed — which some people forget about, and in trying to lift the shaft, strain the coiled oil feed pipe (centre).

14 The actual head nuts can now be undone, commencing from the centre as per the diagram shown alongside.

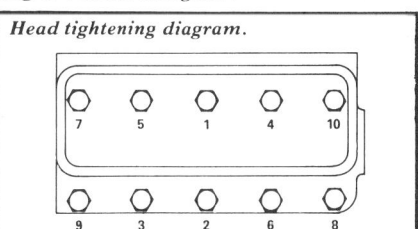

Head tightening diagram.

15 Up she comes — the alloy head is lifted clear of the block.

13 Pushrods are lifted clear, though it's a good idea to rattle the rods first to free the followers at the bottom. Keep the rods in order afterwards by sticking them through holes in a bit of card.

Removing the gearbox and stripping the engine down to evaluate wear. Paul Skilleter continues the story of our 1960 Series III Sunbeam Rapier.

Rapier Restoration!

Last month we showed how removing the cylinder head revealed the results of a bad head gasket leak, but the absence of any serious faults, which means that the head can probably be reassembled with just new valve springs and the normal decoking — valves and guides seemed excellent. Previously the engine had been removed from the car, so that left the gearbox still in place.

To drop the gearbox out was quite a simple matter with the engine out of the way. The front end of the car was placed securely on axle stands, and as can be seen in the pictures, we favour using an old tyre as a precaution against damaging the gearbox casing or bell housing should the box slip off the jack. The removal procedure as detailed in the photographs was quite simple and is just a case of taking care and ensuring that all wires and linkages have been disconnected before the box is actually dropped right down. Note that some wires at the top are

only really accessible when the box on its subframe has been released and dropped down a little.

Incidentally, one tip here is that when undoing snap connectors, pull off different ends if you can so that the two wires are easily joined up correctly when you come to replace them. Or tie a knot in one of the wires!

If you have to take the gearbox out with the engine in place, you have to lower the rear of the engine which means disconnecting the top radiator hose, exhaust pipe, choke and throttle.

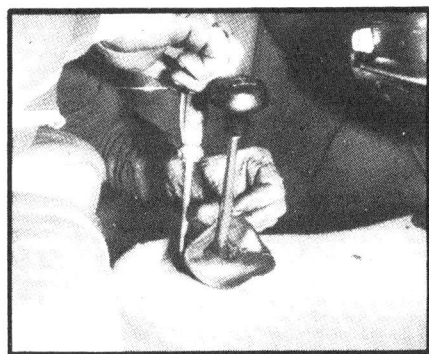

First steps in gearbox removal: dislodge rubber gaiter and unscrew to release gear lever. Oil should be drained at this stage too.

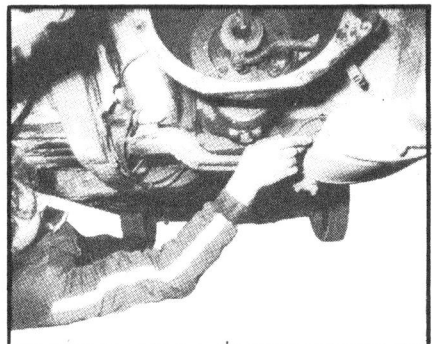

For the sake of undoing a nut, we reckoned it was easier to have the exhaust system out of the way from the start. Having dropped the silencer down, the rear of the system just broke away!

With jack supporting it, the four ½-ins AF bolts securing the gearbox carrier at either end are released; note that front outer bolt also holds bracket for the speedo cable, which must be disconnected from the box.

An old tyre strategically placed will help prevent damage — or even injury — should a mishap occur and the box descend too quickly or at the wrong angle. Gearbox on its carrier is gently dropped a few inches . . .

You also have to remove the prop-shaft rear coupling bolts and remove the shaft rearwards. The engine as well as the gearbox has to be supported too.

We then moved on to stripping the bottom end of the engine, which had already been washed down with paraffin. Everything came off in a straightforward way, and appeared to confirm our impression that this was indeed an 'un-messed about with' power unit. Something will have to be done about the flywheel though because the ring seems to be separating from it — you can see a gap between the two parts. Also the teeth are rather worn in places — and if you want to know why this type of wear is usually uneven, it's because small differences in compression ensures that the engine and thus the flywheel stops in about the same place after you switch off. Our car has probably had at least one clutch replacement, but a generally low mileage is again indicated by the spigot bush which the first motion shaft goes into; often these look egg-shaped as wear builds up, but ours was perfectly round.

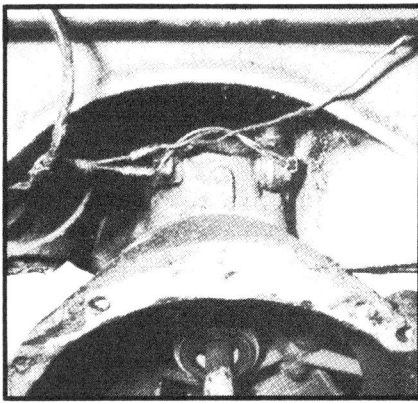

. . . so that reversing light and overdrive solenoid wiring is revealed and then disconnected.

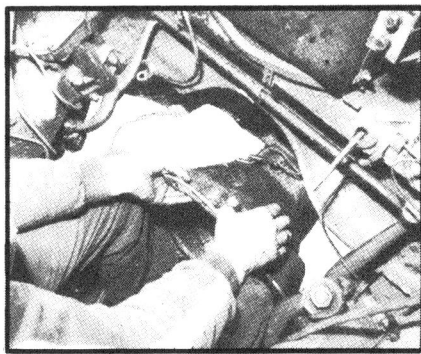

With gearbox parallel with UJ splines, the gearbox can be pulled forward on the jack, with the old tyre under the bell housing just in case.

So we weren't really suprised to find that the crankshaft, like the bores, was standard and showing few signs of wear and no scoring — just a mild, rust-coloured staining in places where the water contained in the oil had got to work on the steel. We're getting the crank accurately checked but think there's every chance that all we'll have to do is fit a new set of bearings. And as it looks as if a rebore and new pistons aren't necessary either, the engine rebuild may turn out to be a very economical part of the Rapier's restoration!

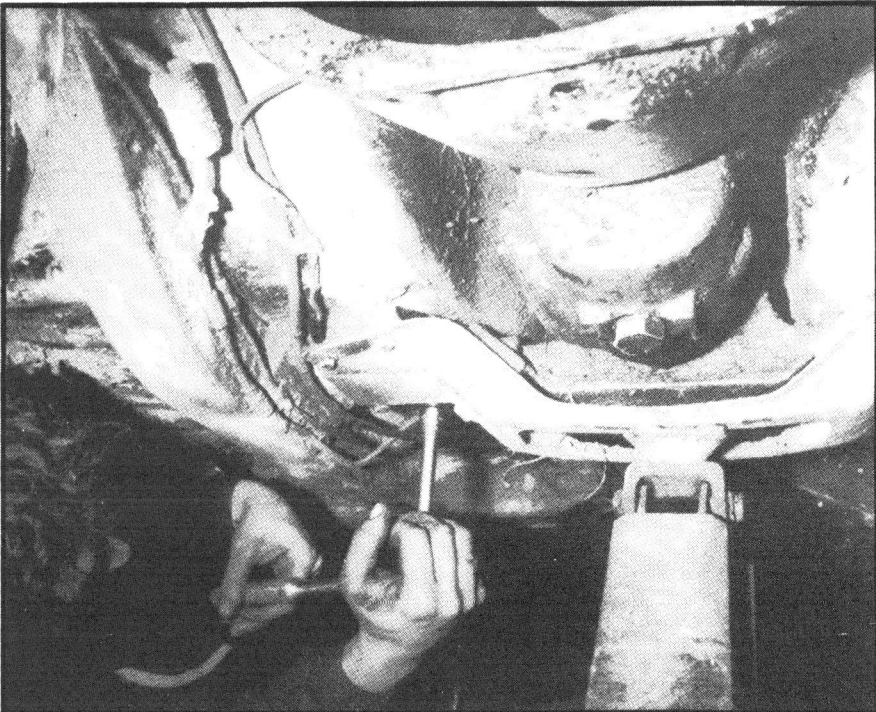

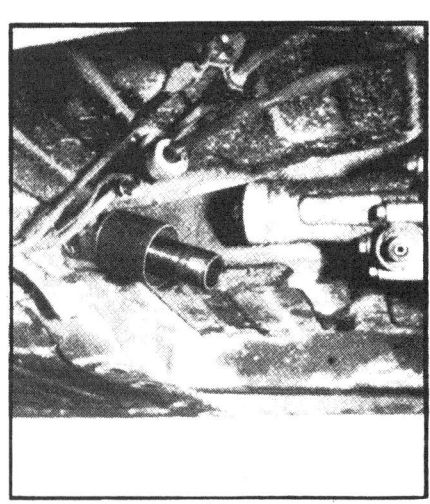

Here the gearbox has just separated from the UJ — and the latter should be coated with grease and covered by a plastic bag to prevent it collecting dirt.

Rapier Restoration!

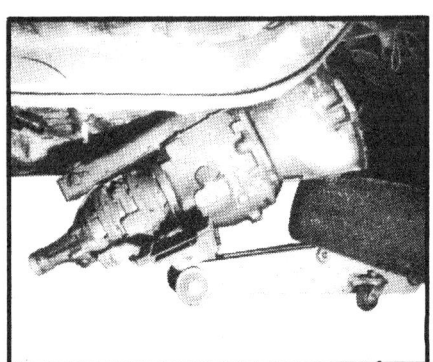

The jack is allowed to slowly descend, carrying the gearbox with it. Box can then be pulled clear of the car.

If you haven't a stud extractor, the cylinder head studs on this engine can quite easily be removed using the locking nut principle. Ensure that the two nuts are tightened together fairly hard first, as shown here.

Ancilliaries like distributor, fuel pump and any hoses left attached to the engine must also come away.

Removal of oil filter assembly disclosed more emulsified oil; side cover is more easily removed with filter away, after which the feed pipe to rocker shaft can be removed too.

Flywheel is held steady by inserting lever in teeth and bracing it against stud while a socket with good leverage is brought to bear on nuts. Flywheel face had escaped scoring from the worn clutch.

Dismantling the clutch showed that the linings were down to the rivets, and some rust due to the car having stood unused for a while.

Starter ring gear teeth were quite badly worn in places — and also, ring showed signs of separating from flywheel.

Removing the flywheel revealed this core plug at rear of block — presumably one that doesn't often fail because it takes a lot of dismantling to get at!

The water pump contained some scale but seemed in excellent condition with no play in the bearings and the correct clearance between impellor and housing.

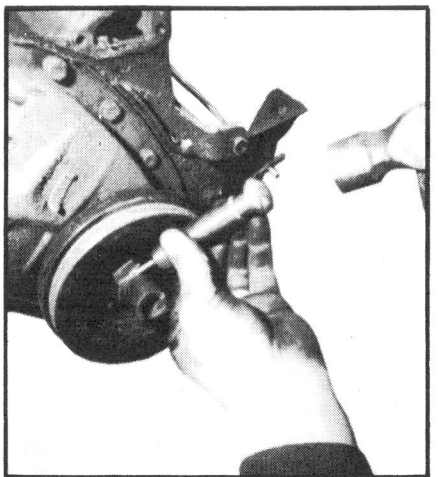

Crankshaft pulley nut usually has to be shifted with careful use of a punch (neater than a chisel), after the locking tab has been bent up. With our engine the pulley was easily levered off afterwards.

Timing assembly can then be levered away, followed by tensioner (after removing split pin), then front plate.

Oil pump was removed by unbolting pipe and pump body from block.

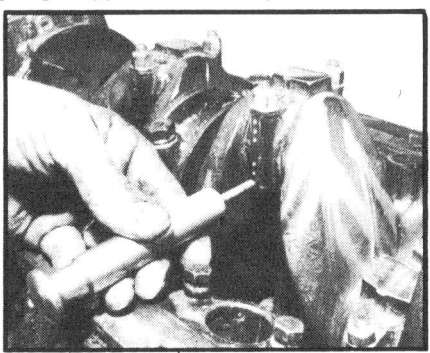

Bearing caps should be marked with punch to ensure correct reassembly. Big end nuts are self locking.

Timing cover is removed (don't forget the centre bolt) then chains and sprockets together after pulling off oil thrower from bottom sprocket, insering a bolt which exactly fits the throw of the teeth to lock assembly as shown, and removing bolt from top sprocket.

Removal of big end bearings disclosed very little wear on the crank, and only slight markings on the bearings themselves.

The main bearings too were in very good condition, though the emulsified oil had produced some discolouration on the crank due to the car standing.

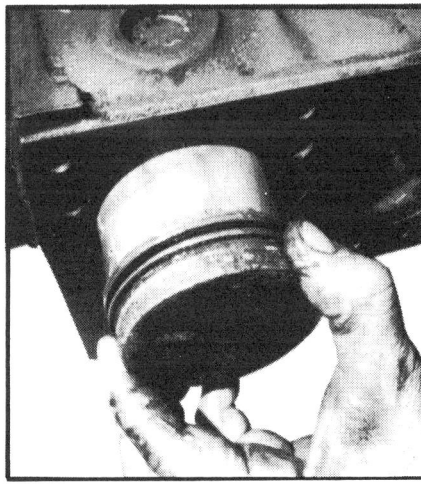

The pistons were withdrawn and we could see the condition of the rings for the first time — the top one was solid with muck but the other two were free and showed very little play.

PARTS

We are just getting to know the parts scene as it affects Rootes Group cars of this period. The Sunbeam Rapier Owners Club (details from David Parrott at 185 Milton Road, Cowplain, Hants) have a small but efficient spares scheme going for members (we joined, naturally), but

Rapier Restoration!

there are few Rootes parts specialists. The Berkshire Sunbeam Alpine Centre (postal address: 37 Tilehurst Road, Reading, Berks.) usually stock exhaust systems, hoses, some suspension parts and so on, although everyone seems to agree that it's R.J. Grimes of Hadleigh Garage, Marlpit Lane, Coulsdon, Surrey (01-668 1455/8, ask for Brian Lewis and mention 'Practical Classics'!) who have the best stocks.

These in fact date back as far as 1935 and even include Rootes commercial vehicles, and were largely built up through Grimes acquiring redundant stock which Rootes/Chrysler/Talbot and their dealers no longer wanted. A few body parts are kept, and it seems certain that most of our mechanical requirements will be met by Grimes without much difficulty. We'll be listing the engine parts we need in a future instalment, together with costs and availability. □

The crank was, as expected, standard; it looks pretty well perfect but will be taken to a machine shop for proper measuring — after binding the journals with masking tape to prevent damage in transit.

The camshaft and bearings seem good (you need a special tool for replacing the latter) but three of the cam followers were badly pitted and will need replacement — probably due to the car having stood rather than wear.

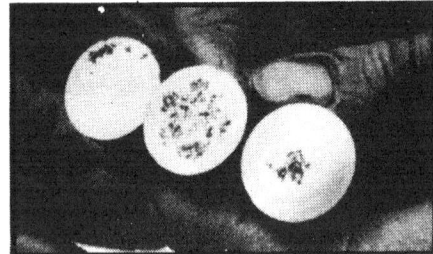

NEXT MONTH
We continue stripping the Rapier in preparation for the body rebuild — and research the question of new wings!

CONTINUED FROM PAGE 14

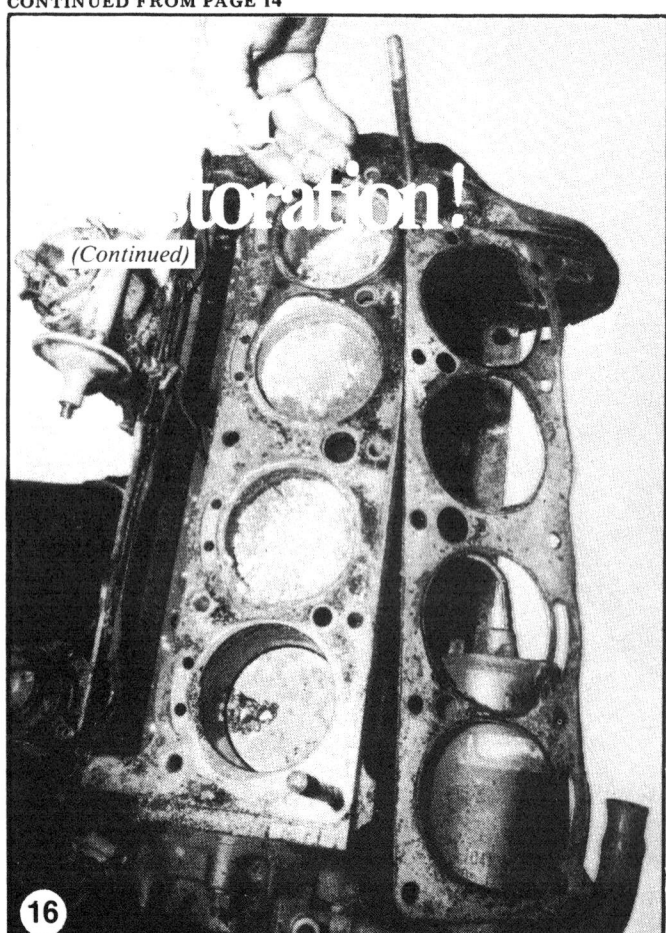

(Continued)

A right mess is immediately revealed — cylinders caked with a whitish deposit. Head gasket alongside, plus marks on the top face of the block, all point to drastic gasket failure.

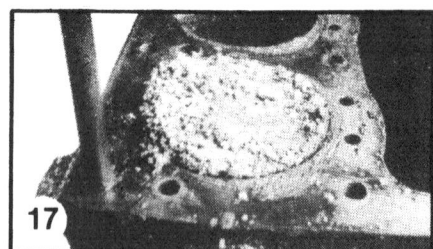

This is number 4 piston at TDC, with a good ¼-inch of congealed anti-freeze on the crown.

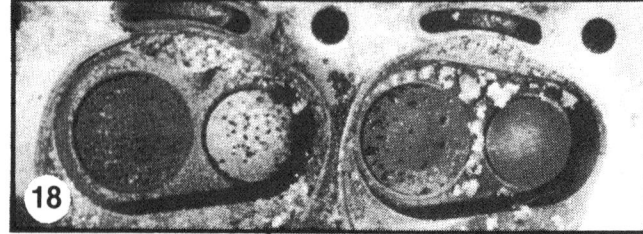

The cylinder head, too, bore all the tell-tale signs of water in the bores, although no actual damage seems to have resulted.

Certainly — apart from the misfire — the unit ran extremely quietly and sweetly before we began the dismantling process. Nor does there seem to be much of a ridge at the top of the bores, so who knows — we may be able to reassemble a very 'standard' engine indeed, though as the Rapier runs a fairly high (9:1) compression ratio it may be advisable to lower this by fitting different pistons, because of the forthcoming reduction of lead in petrol. We'll have to think about that. □

NEXT MONTH
We strip the bottom end and look at bearings, crankshaft and timing gear.

Rapier Restoration!

Thanks to the spell of fine weather in July and early August, we've been able to do all the work on the Rapier outdoors so far. How long this will continue I don't know — but anyway, the car will be going into the workshop after this episode, when the serious bodywork repairs begin.

As a preliminary to the 'heavy stuff', it was necessary to strip the car of all exterior adornments. This may not seem a particularly difficult or time-consuming job, but it is an important stage in a rebuild and one that needs to be treated seriously. Firstly, as this is the last time you'll see the car looking complete, note down anything missing. And as each brightware component comes off, check its

Body strip-down begins as the rebuild of our 1960 Series III Rapier marches on. Paul Skilleter reports.

condition (including any hidden mounting brackets) and whether it needs replacing or rechroming. Also, take care to list what mounting clips or brackets are used, and if you need to find replacements for them too — which isn't always easy, so it pays to start

making enquiries early on. It's also important to label the less obvious parts, and above all to find safe storage for all the bits so they don't get scattered about or damaged while you get on with repairing the shell and the months slide past. It's all too easy to get carried away

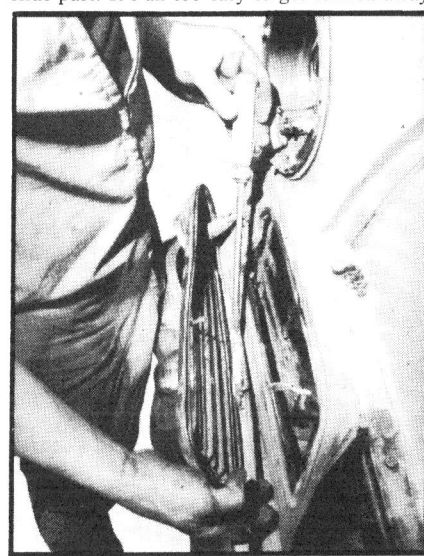

Side grilles are steel and rust due to debris collecting at bottom. Sidelight is contained within the grille.

Centre grille is easily removed by undoing nuts on inside of front panel.

We used the ¼ ins drive Hilka socket extension to get at the nuts hidden inside the front panel, when it came to removing the side grilles.

We released the sidelights by tracing back wiring to snap connectors in engine bay and disconnecting.

Nuts on nearside grille began to seize and it was necessary to hacksaw through the 5/16ins bolt. ▼

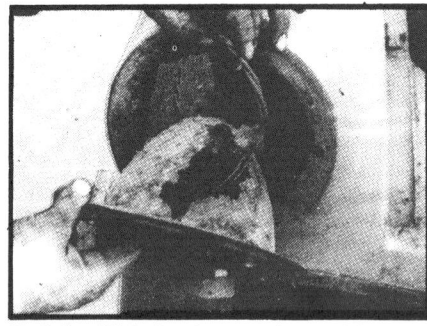

Both headlight bowls were thoroughly rusty, especially the offside one, due to dirt collecting on top in the normal way. Funnily enough, however, the top of the wings at this point are sound.

Side strips or 'body mouldings' are mounted on clips, and are released by easing up from the bottom. Positions of clips can be 'felt' as you go along. Use a sharp piece of wood or plastic/Polythene if car isn't being rebuilt and the paintwork needs to be preserved.

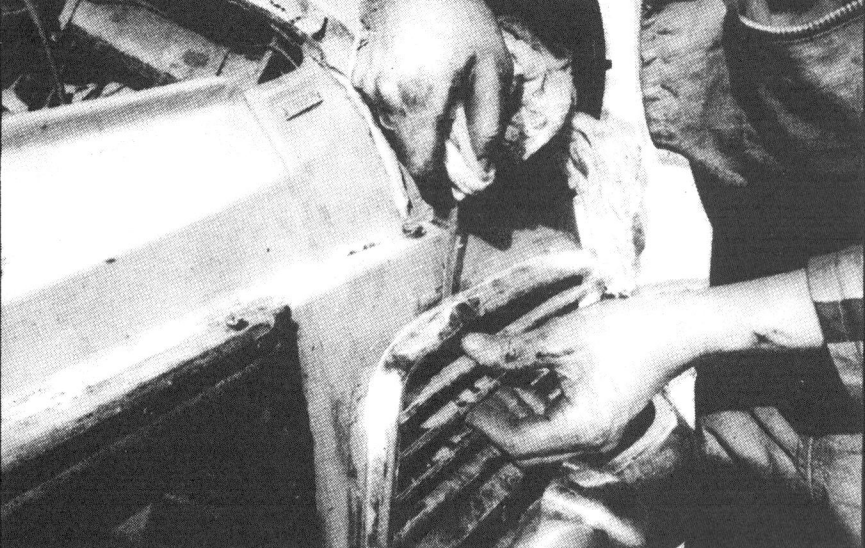

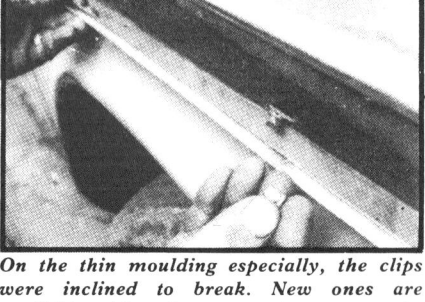

On the thin moulding especially, the clips were inclined to break. New ones are available, although you may have to use the later updated type — but they don't show.

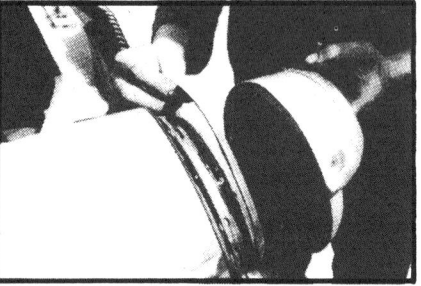

Headlight cowls were removed, taking care to preserve rubber seal. Vintage & Classic Motor Co. have new cowls and light units, by the way.

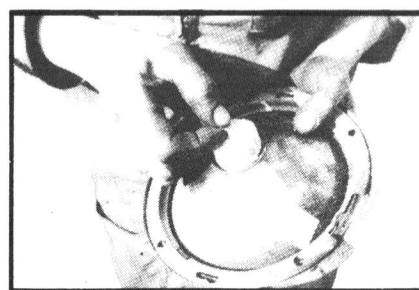

Headlight units were sealed with tape on removal, to prevent deterioration of reflectors which were both good. New ones can still be had though.

Mouldings were bound together with tape and marked 'N/S' or 'O/S' as appropriate — it can save a lot of confusion later!

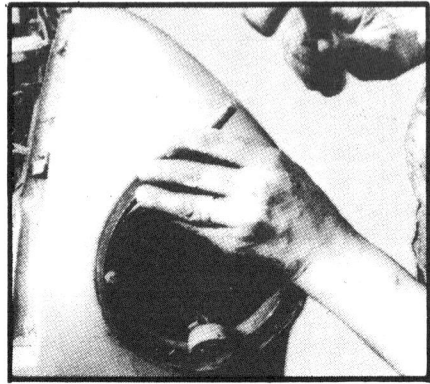

Headlight bowls on this model are rivetted to wing, and require use of chisel to remove the rivet heads. Or you could drill them out.

Bumper removal is straightforward, though a good soaking with penetrating oil a day or so before is a good idea. Bolts go directly into the chassis member projections which also carry the jacking points; no 'crushability' there!

with the stripping operation and not pay attention to details like this — and you could regret it later!

The pictures tell the story of the operation as carried out on the Rapier. No big snags were encountered, and it was at least nice to work on a car which hasn't been crashed or messed about with — no hidden damage or missing or rounded nuts and bolts.

However, we are amassing quite a list of replacement parts needed. As can be seen from the photographs, two new front wings are ideally needed; it is unlikely that actual Rapier wings will be located, but Hillman Minx Series III wings of the same period are the same except for possible small differences where they attach to the front panel (the Minx grille may be wider than the Rapier's). We just missed a pair in our own 'Going Spare' column (a lucky reader acquired them instead)

Rapier Restoration!

We haven't yet begun to strip-out the bulkhead, but we wanted to remove the heater blower unit for closer inspection of the front inner wing. Also it revealed a cracked housing, so we can start looking for a 'new' blower.

so they do emerge from time to time — we believe the part numbers to be 222 1548 and 1549 for the Minx front wings. Any offers? If you're looking for them too, they appear to be selling for around £35-£40 each when they do emerge.

The rear wings are probably in a worse state; again, Minx wings would be better than nothing although they are less suited than the fronts — the Minx being a four-door car, they are rather shorter. Convertible Minx wings would be fine, only you don't exactly stumble across those! Anyway, we'll do the usual autojumble searching and place the odd 'wanted' ad. in various places to see what comes up. The massive Beaulieu Autojumble on Sept. 12 and 13 may well produce something, and as we're having a stand there, we'll have a good chance to look around.

Since the last issue, R. J. Grimes of Coulsdon (01-668 1455/8), who have more old Rootes stuff than anybody, have researched their stock for us and it seems certain that there is a virtually 100% availability on engine parts, and probably most suspension/brake

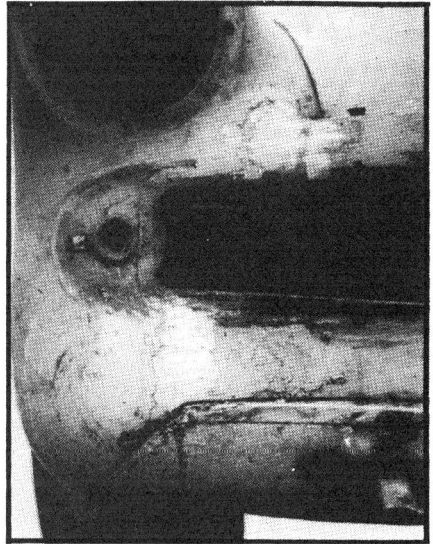

Paint stripper at strategic points revealed the lead loading which covers wing to front panel join. We used Duckhams Jenostrip.

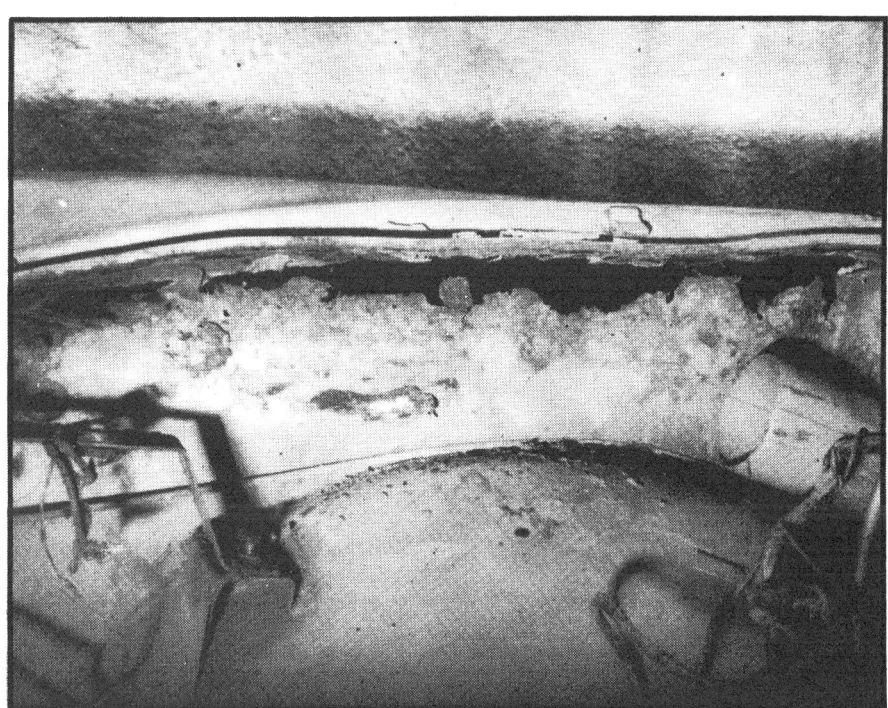

With blower out of the way, the gap between inner and outer wings can be seen clearly. Inner wing should curve up to meet outer wing at the flange, but the top six inches is missing all the way along.

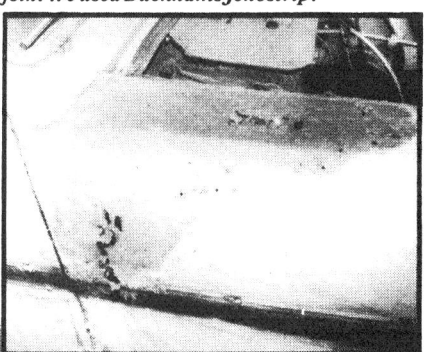

We also paint-stripped the rear top of the front wing to determine the extent of the damage. Verdict — front wings are just about repairable if we really can't find new ones.

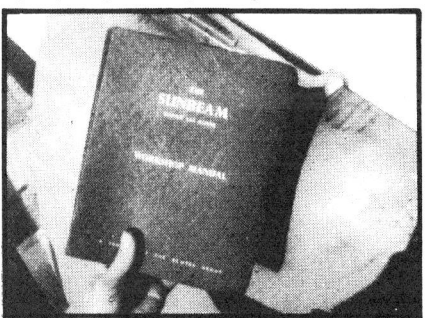

A genuine 'Rootes' workshop manual, still available from Talbot at the time of writing.

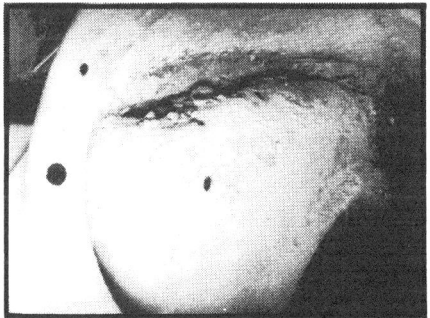

This view through the nearside headlight aperture shows why this happens — the inner wing rises then turns in horozontally to form a beautiful mud trap. Nearside is not so bad.

items too for our type of Rapier (and for Hillmans too). On the body side, things were (predictably) not so bright, though some sills and closing panels are available.

Every Rootes Rapier owner should join the Sunbeam Rapier Owners Club (secretary David Parrott, 185 Milton Road, Cowplain, Hants). We've joined the club's spare parts scheme too, which should help a great deal in rounding up odd bits and pieces, of which the club has a changing selection as things come to light. I'm fairly certain that Talbot dealers must stock various mechanical items for Rapiers too, though you'd need to apply with parts numbers to find out. One thing we did get from Talbot was a workshop manual, part

no. WSM 4, price £5.00 including P&P from Technical Service, Talbot Motor Co. Ltd, PO Box 25, Humber Road, Coventry. This covers Series I-IV Rapiers and Alpines of the same era. Unfortunately the parts book is no longer stocked — the best one is 6601222 which was issued in May 1965 and covered Series I-V models. We hope to pick one up from an autojumble or motoring book dealer in due course.

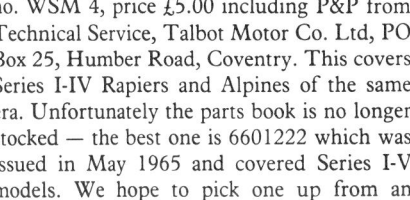

NEXT MONTH

Body repairs commence

23

Rapier Restoration!

Front wings away as the interior of our 1960 Series III Rapier is stripped and the removal of old panels begins.

Two lots of good news about the Rapier project this month; firstly we've secured a pair of new-old-stock front wings and sills for the car, and secondly, dismantling the car is proving that basically it's a very well preserved example. Well, we're about due for an easier job after the traumas of our epic battles with the Minor and the Mini!

As regular readers will know, previous episodes have covered the removal and dismantling of the engine, and stripping the exterior of the car of all chrome, lights and so on. Now it was the turn of the interior, for

quite apart from any need to get at nuts and bolts covered by the trim, it's important to remove carpets, seats and panels to avoid the risk of damaging them during the subsequent rebuilding operations on the bodywork — just one blob of molten metal from the gas torch and you've ruined a perfectly good seat and the risk of total loss through fire cannot be exaggerated. So this preliminary work must be done before ploughing into the metalwork.

The front seats were taken out by undoing the two 7/16" bolts on the outer facing runners, and the two ½" bolts on the inside runners, and lifting the seats out. The rear seat cushion is just lifted out, and the rear squab is removed by pulling it forward to release it

from the two metal flaps at the bottom (we found it necessary to slightly bend these with molegrips) and then upwards to release it from the top two-right-angled clips. The removal of other interior fittings is covered in the picture sequences.

Two things impressed us during these operations — the amount of sound-deadening material employed everywhere, in the form of underfelt and neatly shaped Mutacell pads, and the strength and quality of construction of the shell revealed as the carpets and felt were taken away. Every flat panel has raised 'stress mouldings' and together with the ample size of the various cross members and box sections must have made the car one of the strongest

oration! Rapier Restoration! Rapier Restoration! R

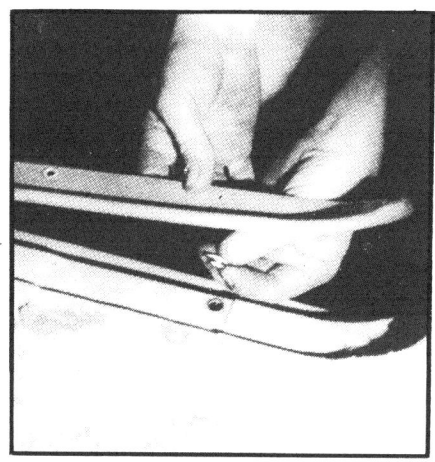

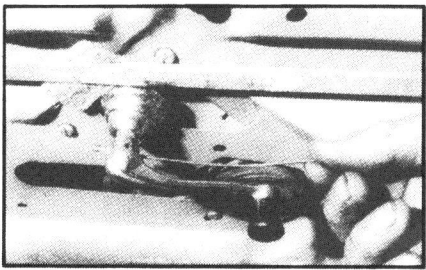

Door/window winder handles are removed by pressing bezels in against their spring, and using piece of wire to push out pin; note alternative hole in shaft and handle, for correct positioning on reassembly.

Alloy kick-plates are removed simply by undoing self-tappers; underneath is a rubber grommeted hole, ideal for rustproofing the sills on a completed car.

from the bulkhead at the top, and this prompted Terry to leave some three or four inches of the front wing in place, attached to the bulkhead, which could be removed later when he could see what he was doing in this area. Likewise, a wide cut round the well-preserved front panel ensured that this was also saved from possible damage. Up the rear side of the wing, the cut was made along the line of rust bubbles which conveniently indicated where an internal panel lay adjacent (because the angle so formed collects mud which causes the rust). It was also the weakest point and thus the easiest part to chisel. The remaining bit of the old wing here, attached by spot welds to the hinge pillar, could be removed with ease later with the bulk of the old wing out of the way.

Of course the above method of working only applies if you *know* you have replacement wings to go on afterwards; if we hadn't found

homework and figure out exactly how the wings were fitted in the first place, and how you are going to put on the new ones. This means looking carefully at the surrounding panels to judge their condition and to avoid unintentionally damaging them as you effect

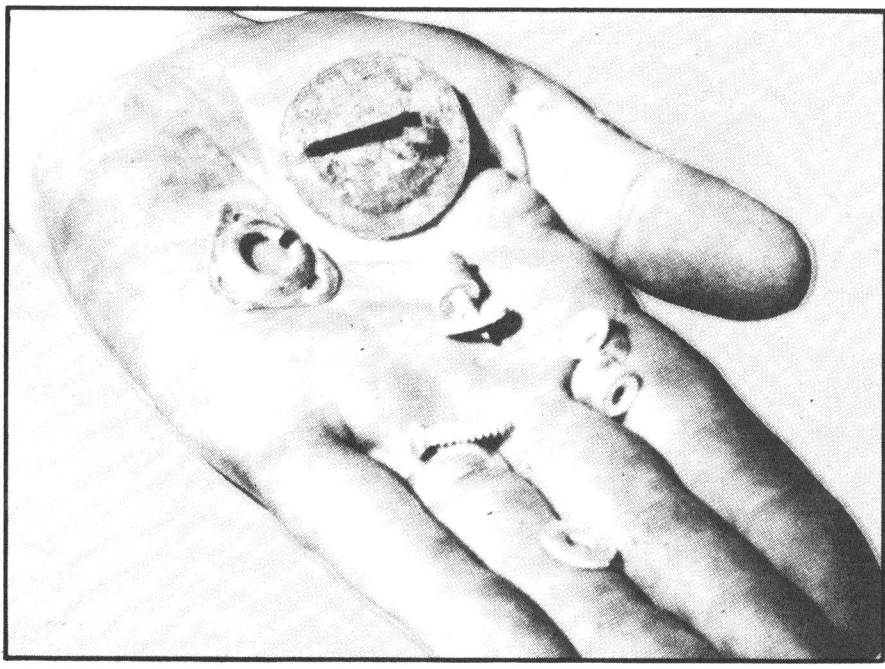

Carpets and underfelt were secured by various types of studs, all carefully retained. Metal disc covers hole in floor instead of the more usual rubber bung.

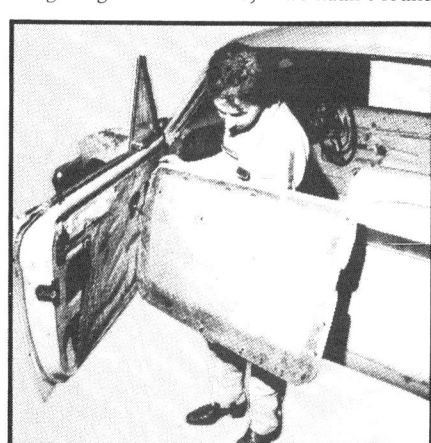

Chrome door catch surround (4 screws) and arm-rest have to be removed before door trim panel can be unclipped, revealing on our car a sort of tarred paper panel designed to deflect water from trim. With panel off, the four screws holding on door capping can be undone.

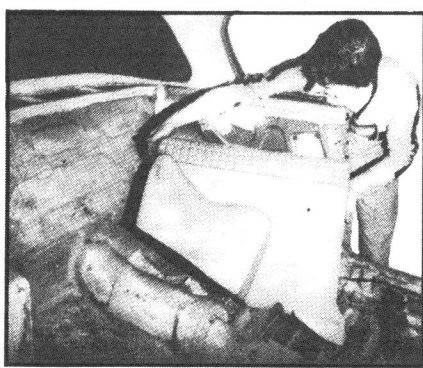

Rear window winder is removed as per front, then rear side trim panell can be unclipped; it's also secured by one self tapper at the bottom under the arm-rest. Parcel shelf is simply unclipped.

and most rigid of its era — possibly explaining why the Rapier did so well in rallying. Traditionally, Rootes cars were always reckoned to have a more 'quality' feel to them than many other mass-produced vehicles, with a better ride and less noise, and this solidity of construction probably shows why. Mind you, the customer did pay for it, both in terms of initial cost and petrol consumption, as the Minx (on which the Rapier is based) was always more expensive than its Austin/Morris and Ford equivalents to buy and run.

So on to the bodywork. As always, before tearing off old panels it pays to do your

the removal of the old panel. With the Rapier, the front inner wings had almost rotted away completely at their tops, where they curve in to meet the outer wing flanges each side of the engine bay. So while the new outer wings themselves would give one guide to where the inner wings would have to be rebuilt out to, Terry decided to play safe and leave the old inner and outer wing flanges together and in place; this was done by cutting the outer wing outboard of this flange on each side, as demonstrated by the photographs.

Then at the rear of the front wings, peering up inside disclosed a box section extension

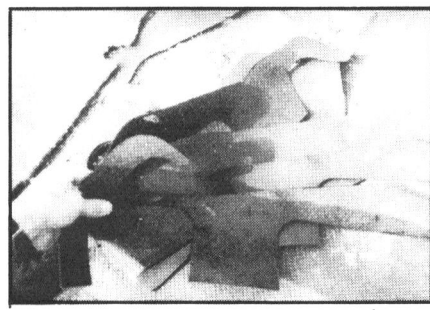

Rootes took a lot of trouble to silence the Rapier — these cut-out sound dampening pads are just some of the sound-proofing material removed from the car. Fortunately all are in good condition and will be replaced, though this type of material can still be bought new.

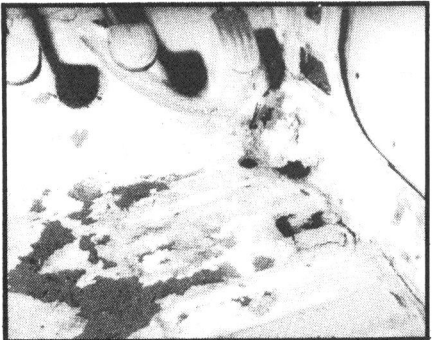

The only rust damage found in the floor pan after removing carpets etc. was in the front outside corners, due to dirt collecting in the holed sills. Inner sill walls are perfect.

Similar rust in the nearside footwell, plates on floor cover hinges on pillar, wiring is for rear loom and runs alongside (not inside) sill.

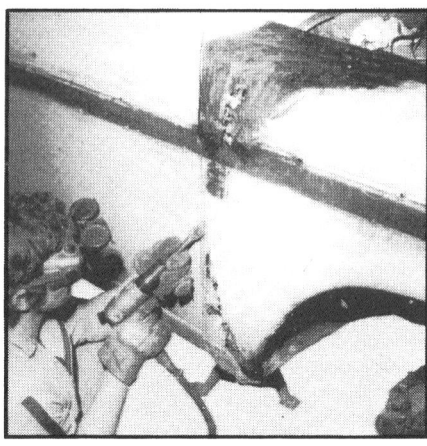

Front wing was only chiselled free after some careful research. At the rear, it was basically a case of following the rust line . . .

. . . and keeping clear of bulkhead which extends under rear of front wing. Air chisel speeds up the work but is by no means essential.

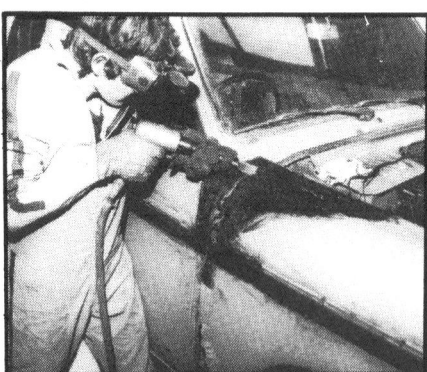

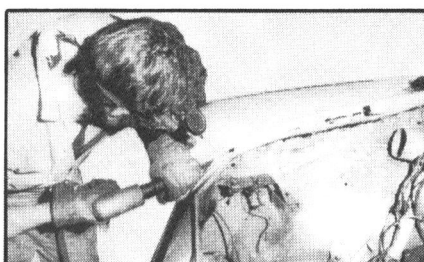

No attempt was made to separate the outer wing from inner wing (which had decayed badly); instead the wing was chiselled free along the outboard, right-angled part of the flange as seen here.

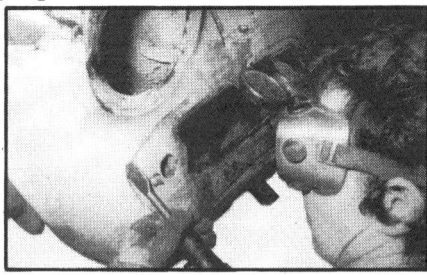

Again, no attempt was made to separate the wing from the front panel where they join, a wide sweep being cut well clear of the apron.

The last cut is made and the wing is lifted clear of the car. Front panel is remarkably well preserved and has been left completely intact.

Tattered remains of the rear of the front wing hangs down as Terry examines the point where sill meets wheelarch. State of inner wing is obvious, and it's the same the other side. Leaving flange in place along top gives a contour to rebuild the inner wing to.

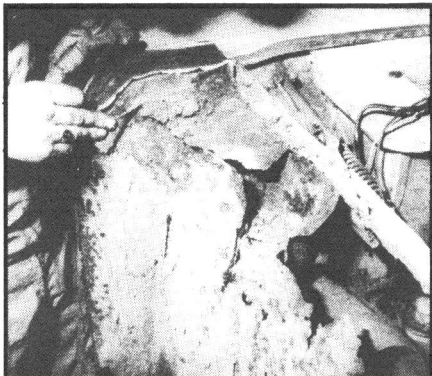

This is where the rear part of the front wing attaches to the hinge pillar/bulkhead. Next job is to carefully drill the spot welds and remove the remains in readiness for fitting-up the new wing.

new wings, we'd have been forced to remove the old ones by very carefully drilling and cutting them off at the original attachment points, a much more time-consuming process. Otherwise, if you have the correct replacement panels, the golden rule is to always make your cuts *within* the old panel, thus avoiding damage to the main structure of the car.

This is why Terry made the top cut to free the old wing well away from the bulkhead — there's a box-like extension which projects forward at this point, though it's well on the way to disintegration. There's some sort of rubber sealing strip at the back too, possibly designed to prevent debris from getting into hinge pillar. A lot of work needed in this area!

As for tools, Terry used a pneumatic chisel to speed up the process, but the routine is exactly the same when using an ordinary hammer and chisel. In both cases a degree of care is necessary, as it is with the other alternatives, a cutting disc on a grinder or electric drill, or the gas torch. The disadvantages of the latter two methods are in the first instance, the inability of the cutting disc to get into some corners or go round some angles (and you must never exert a bending pressure on a disc or it will break with highly dangerous results), and in the second, the possibility of flame damage to unseen parts of the car including wiring harnesses. Cutting with the welding torch (if you even have the equipment!) is better deferred until the outer panels are off and you can see exactly where the flame is going — some panel beaters don't approve at all. More about that later!

| NEXT MONTH |
| We remove the outer sills and begin front-end repairs to the Rapier's shell. |

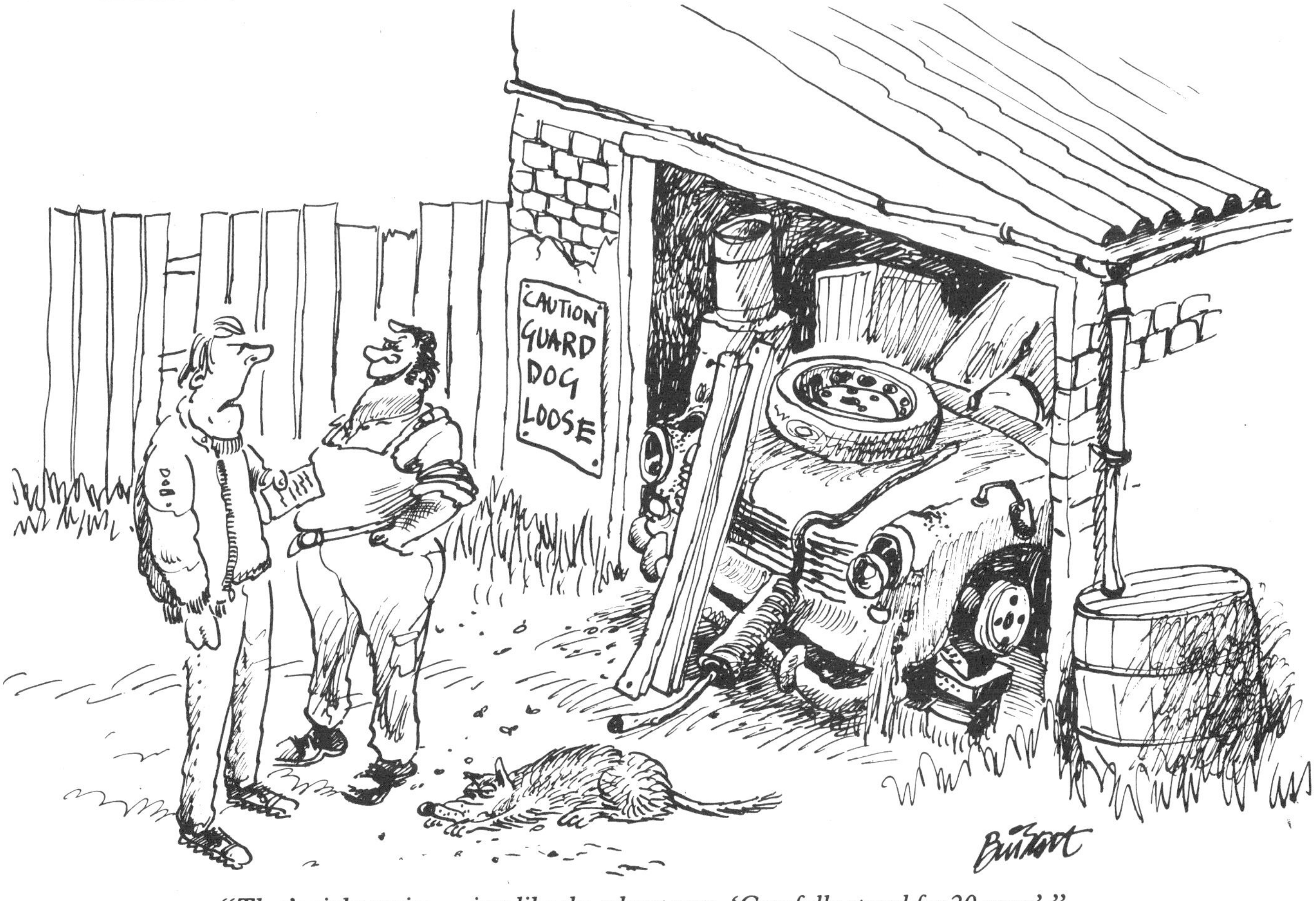

"That's right squire — just like the advert says, 'Carefully stored for 20 years'."

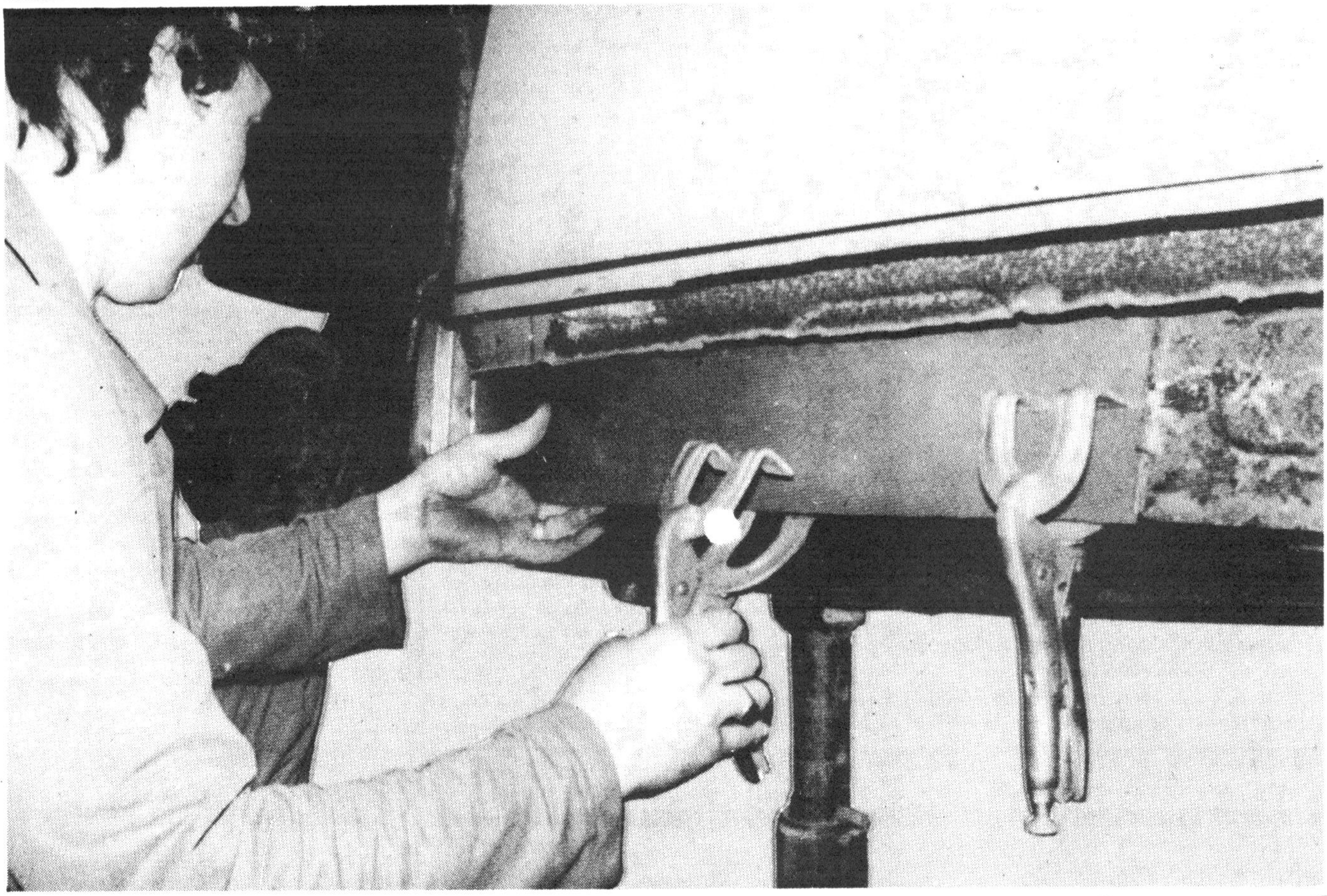

Rapier Restoration!

Work proceeds on our 1960 Series III Sunbeam Rapier as the outer sills are removed and repairs commenced

We left the car last time with the front wings removed and the stripped floor pan having been investigated for rot. This, as we mentioned then, appeared to be restricted to a fairly small area in the front footwells and the adjoining inner sill wall, but to effect proper repairs the outer sill would have to be removed; it was falling to bits anyway.

Terry cut off the outer sill as shown in the picture, in sound metal below the door 'step'. The bottom of the sill needed hardly any cutting (we used a pneumatic chisel but the hand variety works as well), such was the rust, so the body of the outer sill quickly came away. However, revealed was not only the inner sill wall itself but a central wall or membrane,

Rapiers in their hey-day — at the forefront of international rallying.

obviously added to give the shell additional rigidity — I wonder if the Series III Minx had this, or whether it's an extra member used only on the 'pillarless' Rapier and the convertibles? Anyway, the bottom of that was rusted too, so it was cut off about three-quarters of the way up where the metal was sound.

Repairs could then begin on the inner sill wall which abutted the floor. At the front, the inner wall had rusted badly where it projected down past the floor, and the first couple of feet or so had to be cut off at floor level. The floor itself was tackled by cutting out the rotted section, the inward cuts being made along the edges of two of the raised pressings in the floor; using the edges of these provided a stronger point to weld to (and thus helped prevent distortion), and disguised the repair too, making for a neater job.

The small repair panel welded in here was itself given a raised moulding to match those on the floor simply by bending it in the vice beforehand. It was then offered up, the exact area scribed, and the panel trimmed to fit, after which it was clamped firmly in place, tacked in strategic spots, then continuously welded into position. This patch included a

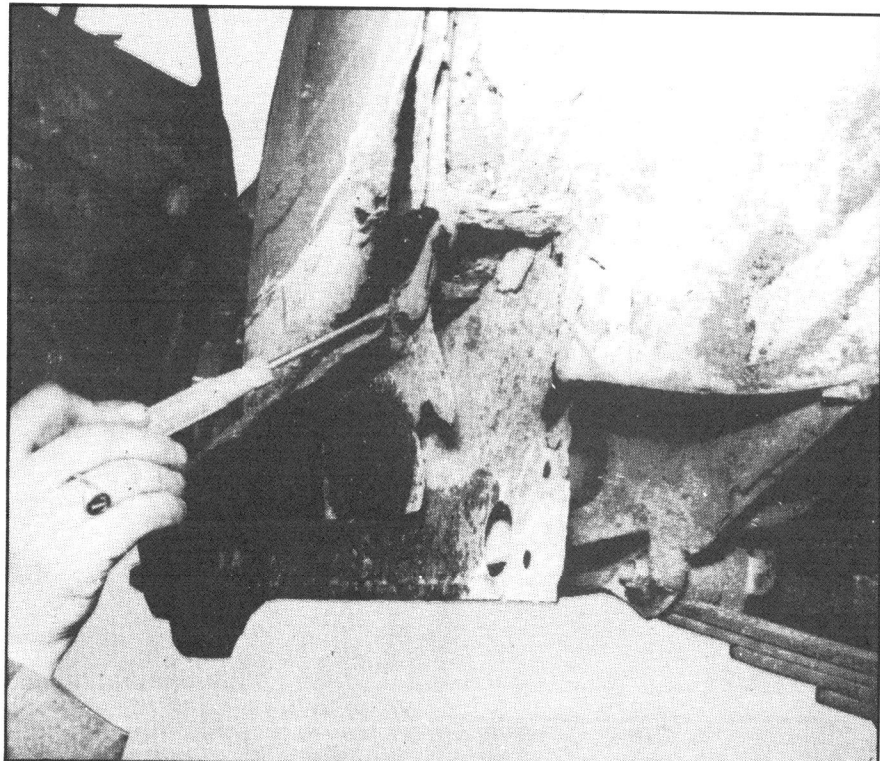

This shows the fairly complex sill structure where it meets the rear wheel arch. It's comprised of inner sill wall (right), membrane, and (now removed of course) curved outer sill. All three meet and are spot-welded at the bottom, giving a triple layer of metal there. Continuation of horizontal door step inside rear quarter panel (where indicated by screw-driver) makes a further box-section member with inner sill wall and membrane.

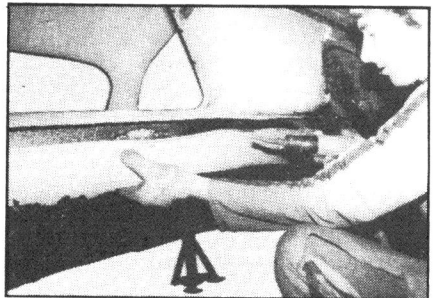

Outer sill was chiselled carefully away about an inch below the door 'step', and at the bottom just above the flange where it meets the inner sill walls.

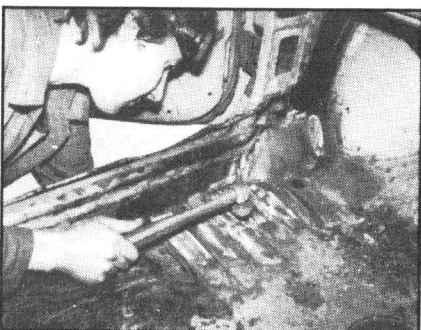

Here Terry dresses the newly welded floor patch. Also visible is the new curved repair section made-up and welded in under hinge pillar.

Removal of outer sill revealed a central membrane or wall; the bottom few inches of this had largely rotted away (Terry holds some of the remains) so the bottom half of the membrane was cut away.

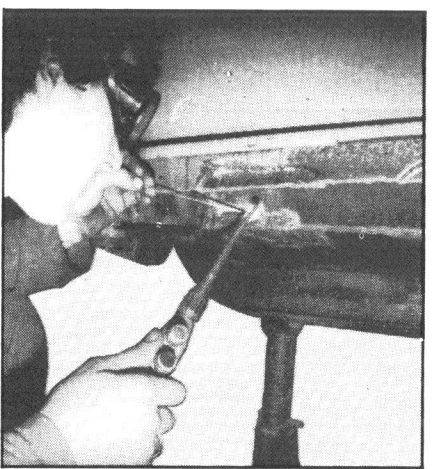

Bottom edge of inner sill wall is stripped of the remnants of outer sill and membrane, and repairs commence with welding in patches to sill wall and floor.

section which was bent at right-angles upwards, to repair the inner sill wall at this point too.

The other repairs in this area included shaping a new rounded section of the sill inner wall under the door hinge pillar; the wall bulges in at this point, a little section of 'floor' also needing to be made up where it curves away from the sill line. Underneath this is a strengthening gusset which on this (passenger) side of our Rapier had completely disappeared, so we shall make one up using the opposite one, which has survived, as a pattern. We'll cover this at a later stage.

The area adjoining the hinge pillar and

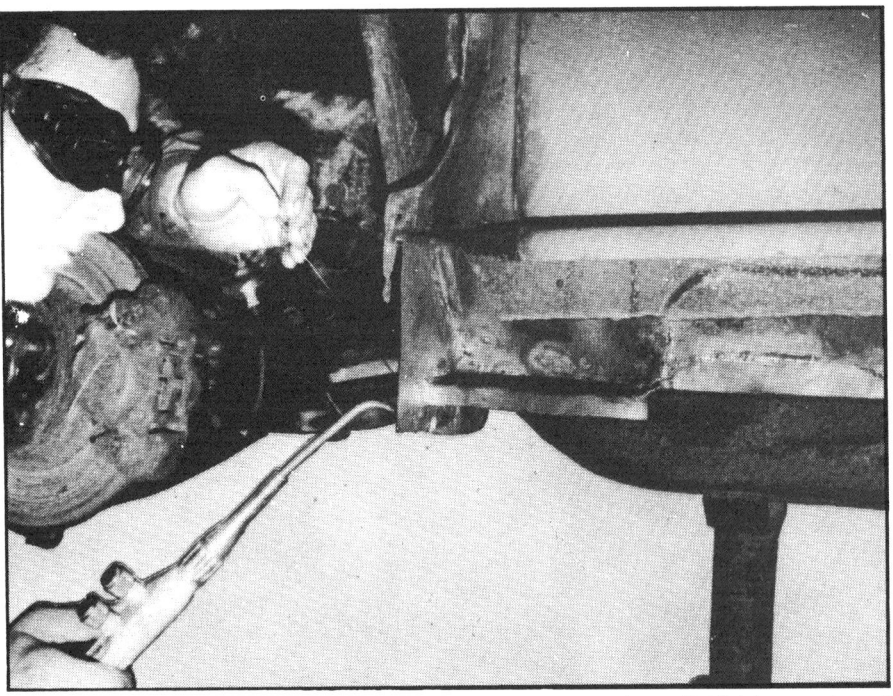

Repaired inner sill wall (right), new curved section under hinge pillar together with its little section of 'floor', and the new closing panel being welded in the bottom of the front wheel arch can be seen in this view.

Meanwhile the remains of the old front wing had been removed from the bulkhead area, finishing the process started last month. With the bulk of the wing cut away, it was easy to drill out the spot welds which secured the wing flange to the bulkhead/hinge pillar.

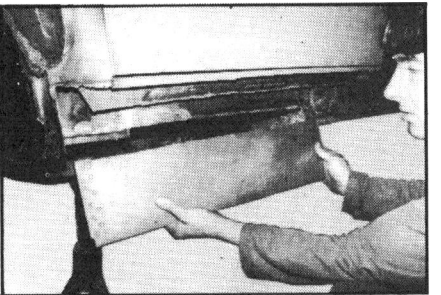

Inner sill wall projects some two or three inches below floor level; at the front this had rusted away and so the remains were cut off at floor level for a distance of about 2 feet. Here Terry prepares the replacement panel, which has had a flange spot-welded to it which will mate up with new closing panel at the front.

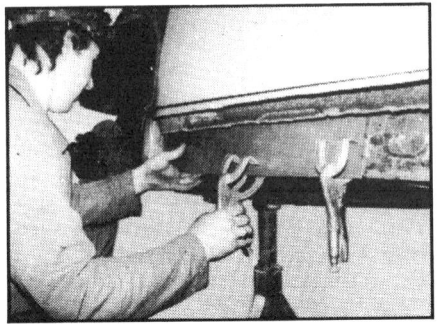

Repair section is clamped up prior to welding in place. Repairs to the inner sill wall wouldn't have been possible had not the central membrane been cut away to allow access.

bulkhead has been cleaned up following the removal of the front wings, some of the latter having been left attached as they were cut off. The spot welds which held these bits on were first located by brushing the parts with paintstripper, and then an electric drill was brought to bear on each one. You only need to drill down far enough to weaken the weld, not as we have seen right through to a hole. Each spot weld can then finally be broken by inserting a lever between the old seam and the body. We used this same technique to remove the old seams left over from the removed outer sill and membrane, which had remained attached along the bottom of the inner sill wall.

The construction of the sill as it approaches the rear wheel arch is quite complex, as can be seen from the photographs, and is next on the list to repair. At the same time we'll be thinking about what to do about the rear wings, the forward edges of the wheel arches being rather badly rusted. As it appears that we aren't going to be able to locate any new rear wings, it looks as if we'll have to improvise with either sections cut from the old front wings (the flares look about right) or with repair sections made for other cars. We shall see; meanwhile, we've ordered a number

of useful parts from R.J. Grimes (Coulsdon) Ltd, Hadleigh Garage, Marlpit Lane, Coulsdon, Surrey (tel: 01-668 1455/8) who are the country's leading Rootes stockists, and from the Sunbeam Rapier Owners Club which of course we joined. These items will be listed when we come to use them.

As an experiment, our new front wings are offered up to the shell. There's some way to go yet before they can be fitted, the inner front wings in particular needing a lot of repairs.

NEXT MONTH
Inner front wing repairs, and
a further look at those rear wings.

Rapier Restoration!

We explore fitting inner wing panels as progress on the complete rebuild of our 1960 Series III Sunbeam Rapier continues. More news from Paul Skilleter.

Having sewn up much of the Rapier's nearside floor, we then turned to the much-decayed inner front wings. And here we have a confession to make — thanks to Mr. John Butcher of Norfolk (tel: 0603 868854) who deals in all sorts of obsolete stock, we managed to acquire a pair of brand new, factory inner wing panels. These are like hen's teeth but I'm afraid that we couldn't resist the temptation to use them on our Rapier despite the fact that few other Rapier owners will be able to find such things — it's pure luck that these turned up out of the blue. However, in order to play fair we have taken templates from the new inner wings and in a later episode will be showing you how to make repair sections for this area.

We found that it was relatively easy to fit an inner wing panel to the Rapier, which of course is identical to the Minx at this point. Having established what the new panel spanned (in fact it goes all the way from the front panel to the door pillar) the old inner wing was cut away, starting by chiselling all round the curved section of the wheel arch radius. At front and rear, the old panel was released by drilling the spot welds, though the part that ran past the inside of the door pillar was left attached as it was good.

We found some rot on the front panel, above the nearside radiator grille aperture and previously hidden by the flange of the outer wing; this was easily repaired by a small patch, however, after cutting away the affected metal. The flanges on the front panel to which the opposite numbers of the new inner wing panel met up with were good, as they were at the top rear, and just needed dressing with hammer and dolly and cleaning up. The curved part of the wheel arch was in perfect condition, except for a tiny hole near the door pillar, so this was

Another shot from the files — a Rapier in full cry on the Alpine Rally.

This, if you remember, is what the original inner wing area looked like immediately after removing the outer wing; it shelves over on top to form an ideal mud trap which has led to the rust holes visible.

Before attempting to cut too much away from the door pillar, it was necessary to remove glove box by undoing two small screws on bracket on door pillar under dash panel, and bolt at other end of supporting bar near heater. A metal tab behind this bolt needed straightening too allowing cardboard to be released.

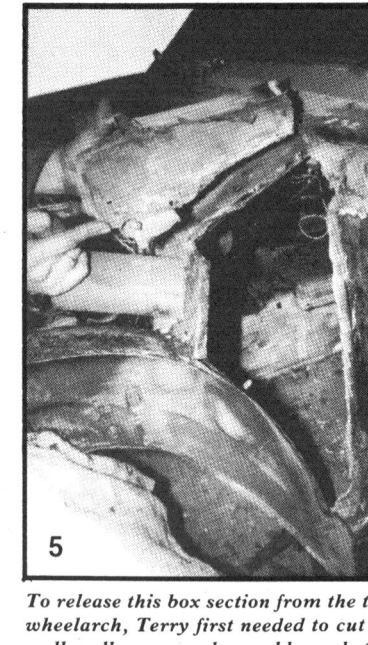

The old inner wing where it joined the door pillar was cut out a bit at a time, taking care not to damage the loom which runs inside the door pillar.

The old inner wing was removed in stages, cutting round the wheel arch and at either end, having established where the new inner wing will join.

To release this box section from the top of the wheelarch, Terry first needed to cut its outer wall well away so he could reach the inner seams.

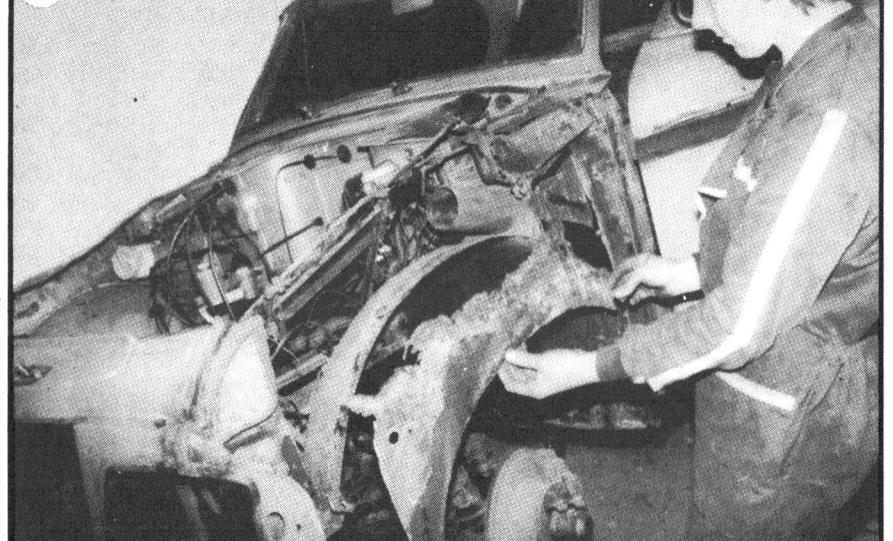

All seams and edges which the new panel will adjoin were dressed and cleaned up.

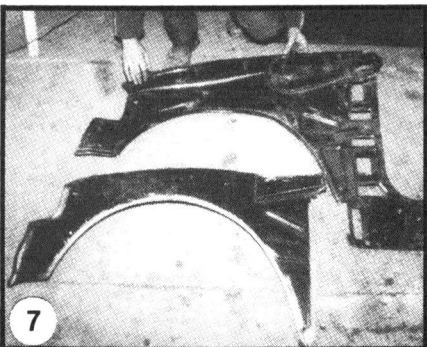

The replacement panel carries right over to and along the inside of the door pillar, but as the original was sound at that point, we cut it so that it joined actually at the leading edge of the door pillar. Where the cut was made is shown by this comparison with the complete inner wing of the opposite hand.

CONTINUED ON PAGE 72

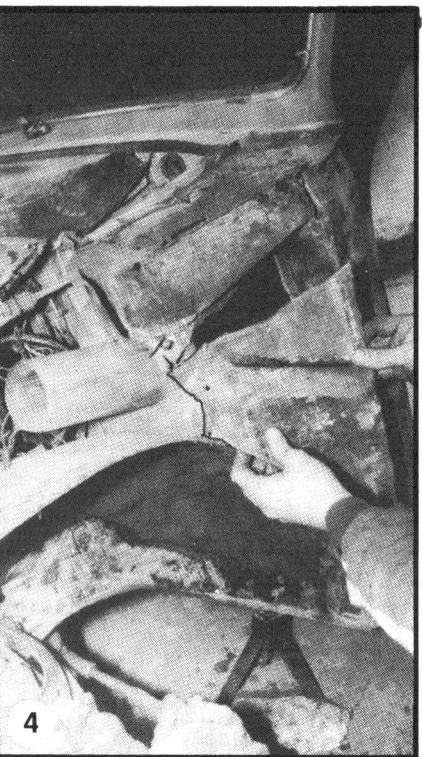

Rapier Restoration!

Quite often during a bodywork rebuild you are faced with the problem of not being able to find a replacement panel off-the-shelf anywhere for your particular car; this happens even with very popular 'classics'' which are well served by specialists, and of course the situation is much worse with less-fashionable cars for which it has not been worth anyone's while tooling-up to make reproduction panels. The Rootes Sunbeam Rapier is a typical example and we ourselves have run up against several blanks.

For example, as disclosed in previous instalments the Rapier's sill structure consists of an outer sill, a central 'diaphragm', and an inner wall. We found a set of reproduction outer sills, but needless to say, no inner diaphragms. We could have replaced these with a simple flat steel panel but we rather wanted to retain the pressings which add strength to the diaphragm. However, we recalled that the MGB also has a central diaphragm with similar pressings in *its* sill assembly, so we popped over to the MGB Centre at Redditch and obtained a pair of these — which indeed do the job.

The MGB diaphragms were cut to fit the Rapier and proved adequately deep with just a short extra length needing to be added at the rear end, plus a strip at the front. They were

MGB parts, and bits of the Rapier's front wings used for the rears, all feature this month as our 1960 Series III car receives more attention. Paul Skilleter reports.

then welded into place as shown in the pictures.

It was then a case of working from the front back in order to fit the outer sill. Unfortunately our new Rapier front wings turned out to be Minx ones with a sidelight housing built in at the front, where on the Rapier there is a simple smooth curvature meeting the front panel (which is a separate part). Even more unfortunately we had broken one of our own rules and cut the old front wings off before the replacements had arrived and could be confirmed as being the genuine articles, which meant that after we'd removed the sidelight housing from the Minx wing, a gap existed. Still, shaping a piece of metal and fitting it should make an interesting story later on!

Apart from this, fitting the new wing was plain sailing, and once in place it was possible

to offer up the new outer sill, again working from the front backwards. The repro outer sill wasn't brilliant, in that where it curved over at the top the radius was a little too tight compared with the original, and also the resulting flange was a little proud (i.e. it sloped

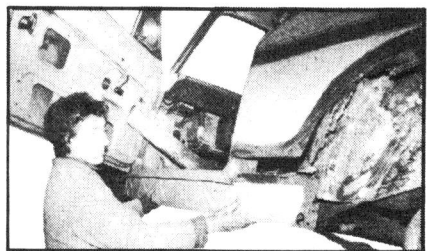

The MGB part we'd decided to use for the internal diaphragm or 'middle' sill wall is offered up, having been trimmed to fit.

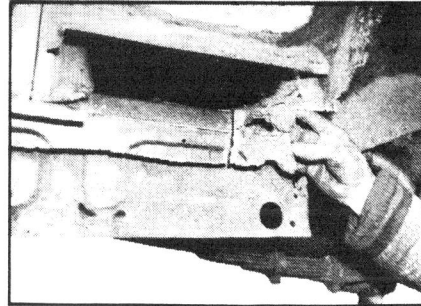

Meanwhile in preparation the sill extension which meets the rear wheel arch has the rust cut out of the curved section adjacent to the arch.

tion! Rapier Restoration! Rapier Restoration! Rap

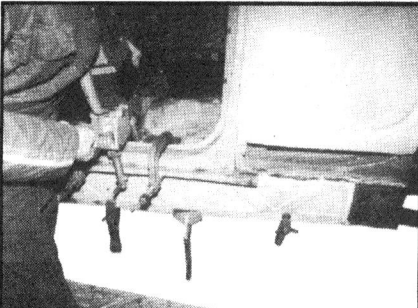

With the new rear portion of the sill extension made-up and fitted, the MGB diaphragm was spot- and gas-welded into position. Under the door aperture, enough of the original diaphragm was left to overlap the new one at the top, so that the two could be spot-welded together.

The front outer wing was offered up next, before moving on to the outer sill. It mated up nicely with the new inner wing flange but being a Minx wing, needed modification at the front.

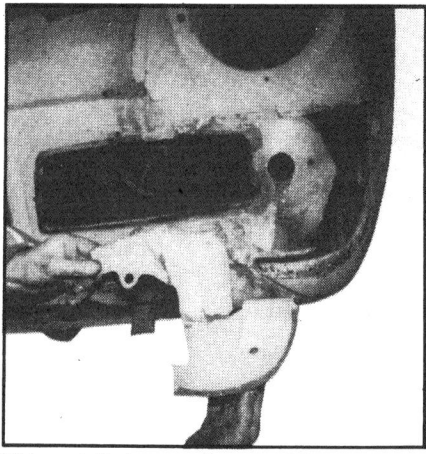

This entailed removing the Minx sidelight housing by drilling the spot-welds at the bottom of the housing, and cutting at the top. Shaping the metal to fill the resulting gap looks like being quite tricky!

The same area viewed from below with the rotten section cut away; this repair is only possible if you cut away the outer panel as we've done . . .

. . . though limited access is also available via removable (self-tapped) plate on inside. Note sound deadening material on exterior side panel — easy to set fire to especially if you haven't removed the interior trim at this spot and are working 'blind' from the outside only.

up) of the part of the original door step it was to overlap. However, we are confident that a good fit will be obtained with a little dressing with the hammer.

Before the car had been stripped we noted that the sill lay proud of the door line as original, particularly at the rear, so this was borne in mind when the new sill was offered up. It is worth examining your rebuild project very carefully before starting work (or looking at an original example if yours has already been got-at) and taking note of points like this, otherwise you may attempt the impossible when fitting new panels later. For the same reason it's a good idea to rebuild just one side

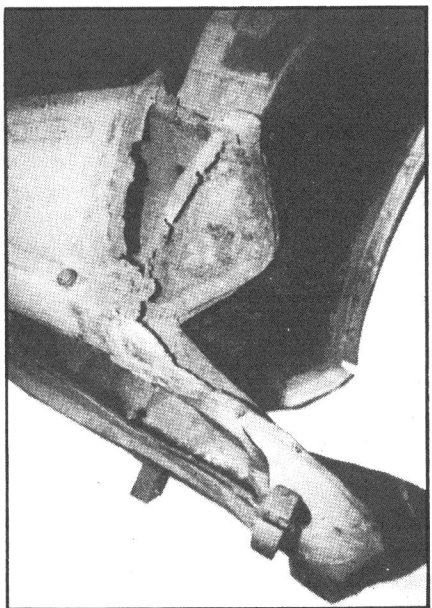

The outer sill was then clamped along its length, top and where it meets the centre diaphragm and inner sill wall at the bottom.

Replacement sill is made to overlap the original where it runs under the door aperture to form a step; the radius arrowed on the new panel was a bit sharp compared to the original, which was more rounded at this point. Note that new sill was cut where door pillar (also cut and bent back slightly) overlaps it; it will be gas-welded to the remaining part of the existing sill here, then pillar bent back into place and also gas-welded, to provide a very strong point to withstand stresses from door being slammed.

This is the same place viewed from the top, showing the rusted flange on left which needs repairing before the new outer wing is finally welded into place.

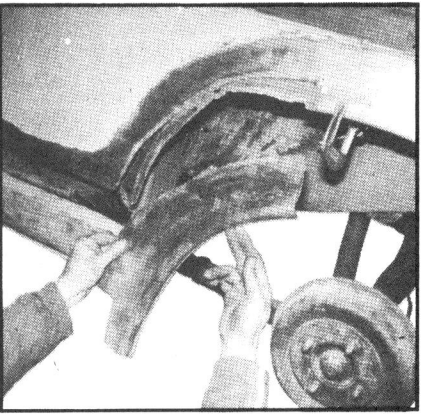

The rear wheel arch was stripped, and the rusted section removed by hack-sawing through it — with the repair section clamped to it on top so that it was automatically cut to the right length.

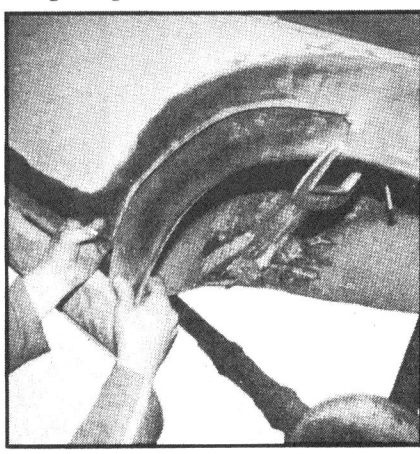

The 'new' wing lip in place; it will actually be fitted compete with a new section of inner wheel arch, a procedure which will be covered next month.

of the body first so you can always refer to the other to see how the panels fit together and what the gaps should be.

Another item we couldn't find for the Rapier were rear wings — Minx or the genuine article. Then Terry spotted that the front wing lips appeared to be much the same shape as the rears, and a bit of measuring confirmed that they indeed were almost exactly similar. So as shown in the picture sequences, we've created repair sections for the rear wings by cutting out the relevant parts of the front wings, which were fortunately in excellent condition at this point — a dodge which seems to be working well! □

NEXT MONTH

Completing the rear wing repairs, and finishing outer sill and front wing fitting.

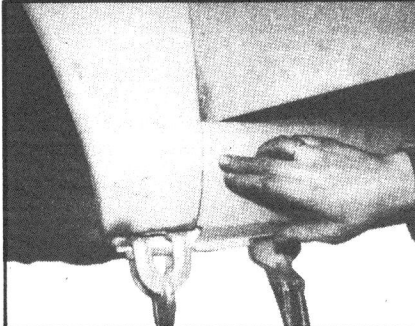

The correctly positioned front wing then provides the starting point for fitting the outer sill, which slots behind it as shown.

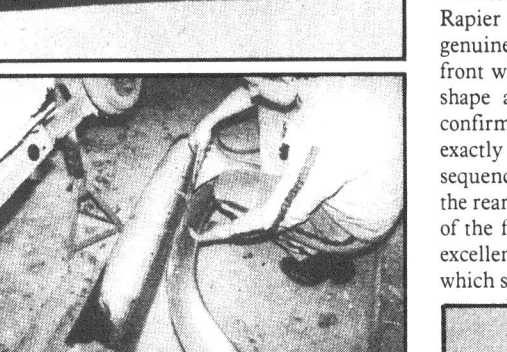

Meanwhile, rear wheel arch repairs have commenced with cutting out the lip from the old front wing to use as a repair section.

Rapier Restoration!

Wing and sill fitting techniques as we carry out these jobs on our 1960 Series III Sunbeam. More news from Paul Skilleter.

The nearside front wing and sill were trial-fitted as shown last month; then came the job of actually welding them in place, and this turned out to be unexpectedly tricky.

First of all, the sides of a Rootes Rapier (and no doubt its Minx/Gazelle cousins too) have a distinct curvature from front to rear, i.e. it bulges out near the middle. Our 'pattern' outer sill did not, unfortunately, contain this shape and was straight from front to rear. Additionally, the sill tucks under markedly at the rear, which means the cross-section of the sill should flatten out at this point; needless to say ours didn't. It was thus a case of persuading the sill to follow the line of the car, which it did eventually using the door 'step' (which it over-lapped) to help it conform

lengthwise, and fillets cut in the end flange to allow the top/bottom curve of the sill to be flattened and thus provide a little extra depth so that it would reach when pulled in at the bottom, as on the original.

This episode highlights the necessity of being able to refer to pictures or examples of original cars when undertaking a rebuild, because logically, the sill looked as if it could simply be popped onto the car with no complications. Had we not been able to look at pictures of new Rapiers (thanks to illustrations in the Sunbeam Rapier Owners' Club newsletters!) we might well have attempted to achieve a straight line fore-to-aft, which would have been completely wrong. Also, we noted both from pictures and from our own car before we started dismantling, that the door,

although curved too, did not follow the outward curvature of the sill entirely but at the centre was distinctly inset. Had we not been aware of this we might have spent untold hours trying to make the two match exactly! Another point to note on the Rapier is that the top sill line is continued right back to the rear wheel arch by means of a small rounded shoulder — i.e. it is not filled flush with the side panel.

The rear wing repair section, cut from the offside *front* wing as explained in previous instalments, was brazed into place with little trouble and thus got us over the problem of the very rotten rear wing lip. We decided not to fit it complete with a section of inner rear wing, this latter being easiest to fit separately. It should be noted that the wing lip or moulding on the rear fades out *before* the sill — another fact which emerged from examining pictures carefully because our own car had been so fudged at this point that you couldn't tell how it was supposed to be.

Fitting the front wing also brought complications. Clamped into position during the trial fit, all seemed to be well with the correct gap between the wing and leading edge of the door, while at the front the altered Minx wing conformed nicely to the front panel. The

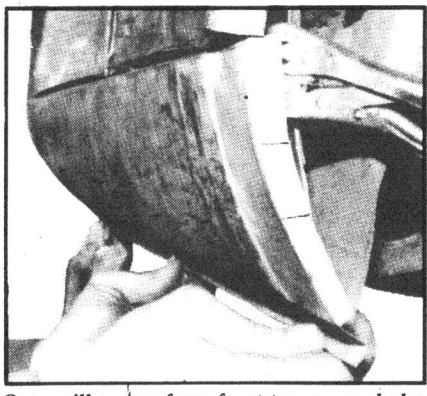

Outer sill curves from front to rear, and also pulls in quite sharply at the bottom rear (where Terry is pressing it in). Note fillets cut in flange to assist this.

Side panel is then closed-off by brazing in a mild steel section cut to shape; side panel was first rebated or 'stepped' so that new section lies flush. Where Terry is brazing at the bottom, the braze is kept under the section (which has been given a turned-in edge) to maintain the small 'shelf' which runs right up to the rear wheel arch.

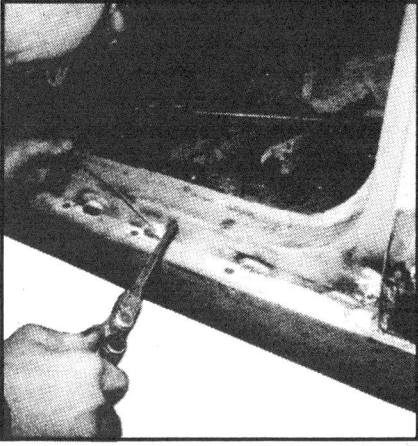

Continuous welding along the top of the sill would have resulted in a lot of distortion, so 1 - 2 ins of weld are laid at about 3 ins intervals instead. Braze will be run into the gaps left, and the process completed with lead-loading.

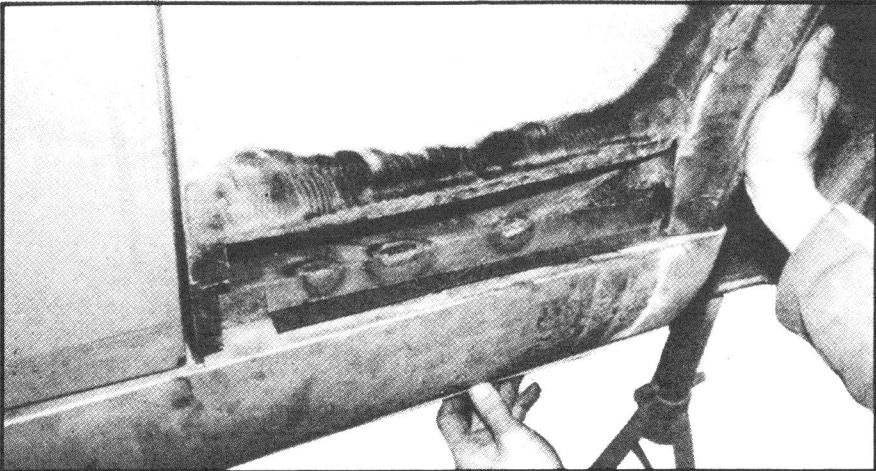

Rear wing lip moulding ends just before it meets the sill. 'L' shaped length of steel has been made up and fitted to additionally secure flange of outer sill to inner structure which is later closed-off.

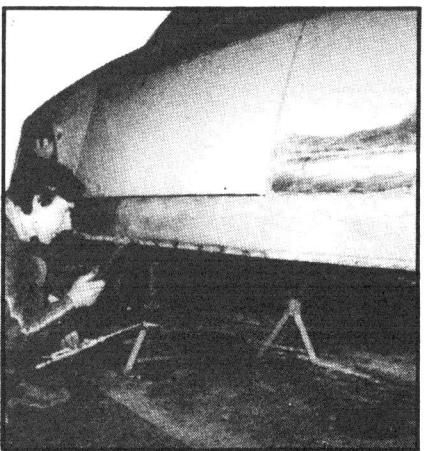

Finally, the bottom flange of the outer sill is plug-welded to the flanges of the middle and inner sill walls (which represented too great a thickness for the spot welded to reliably cope with) and dressed straight.

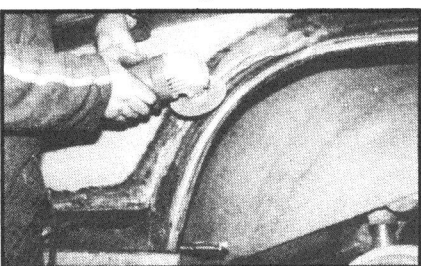

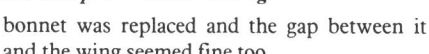

Wing repair section is spot-brazed to car, and linished prior to lead loading.

bonnet was replaced and the gap between it and the wing seemed fine too.

Accordingly, Terry tacked the back of the wing to the door pillar/bulkhead having achieved the right gap between door and wing. However, when he then self-tapped the wing to the inner wing all the way round, he noticed that the gap between *door* and wing had widened very considerably. Making the outer wing conform to the curvature of the inner

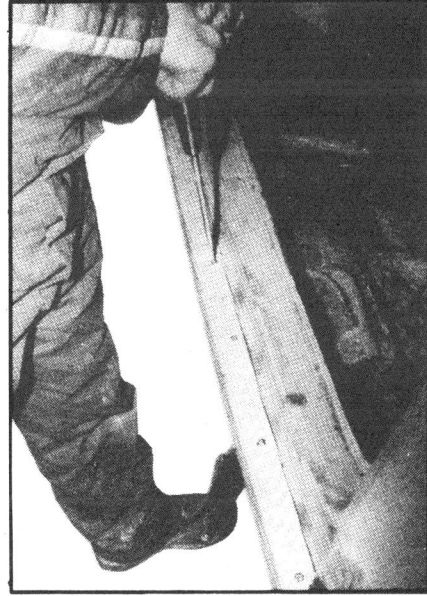

Meanwhile the outer sill has been secured by self-tapping screws where it overlaps the door step, the latter having been used to make the replacement sill conform to the fore/aft curve.

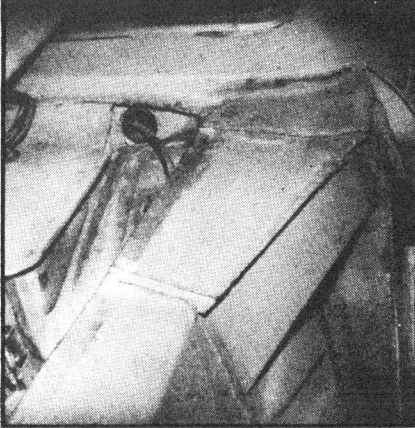

Moving on to the front wing, repairs to the inner rear wing adjacent to the scuttle were completed by boxing-off this stiffener at the top.

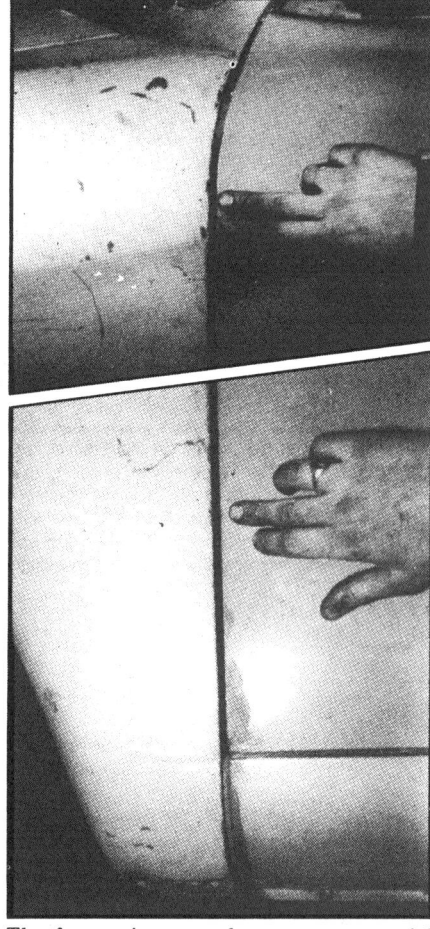

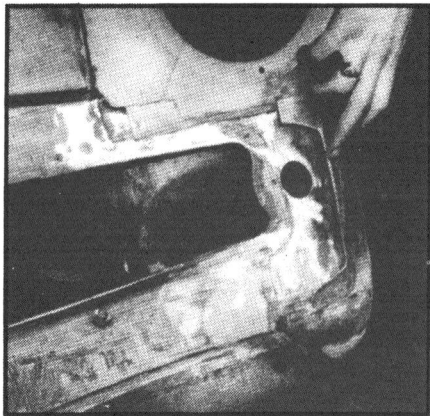

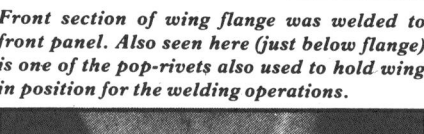

Front section of wing flange was welded to front panel. Also seen here (just below flange) is one of the pop-rivets also used to hold wing in position for the welding operations.

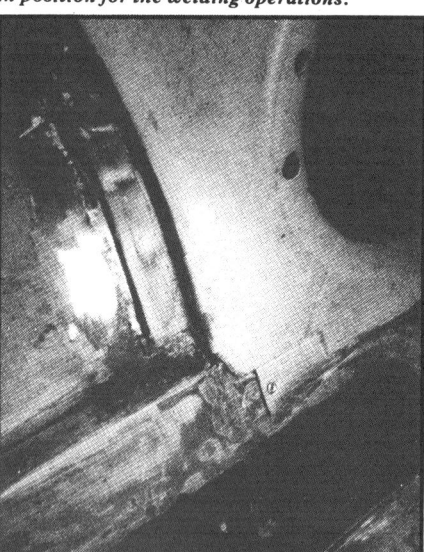

This shows the new section made-up and fitted to the wing to cover gap left by the Minx sidelight housing which had to be removed. The new piece overlaps a little of the existing front panel, adjacent to screw hole for offside grille.

Wing and inner wing flanges were held together by self-tappers then spot-welded together (after some hassle — see text!).

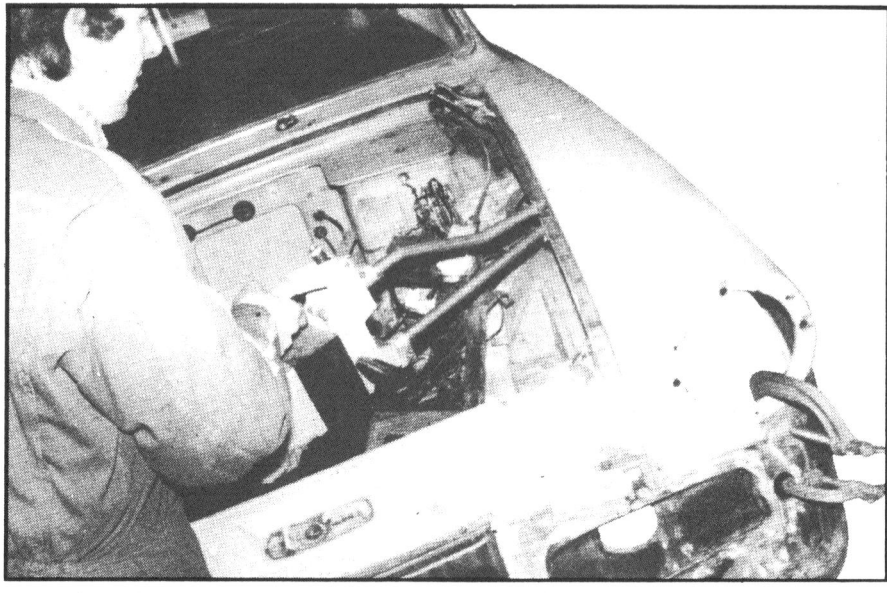

The front wing was then once more trial fitted, and the correct gaps in relation to the bonnet (which was replaced) and door were checked. The gaps on these Rootes cars are quite wide, something in the region of ¼ ins.

View of the inside top rear corner of front wing/bulkhead. Where the wing met the bulkhead at the rear, Terry brazed on tabs so that clamps could be used to pull the two together —there was no other way to do it. The wing was then welded at intervals to bulkhead/door hinge pillar.

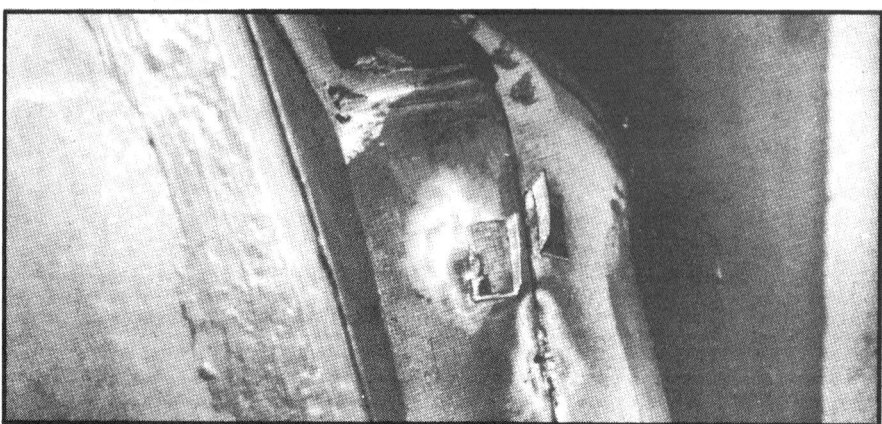

wing had caused it to pull forward. So the wing had to be taken off and the process begun again — and this time he set the gap between wing and door very tight, so that as the wing was self-tapped along the inner wing flange, it pulled back to exactly the *correct* gap. Experience which will be put to good use when the other side is done!

NEXT MONTH

How to make templates so that you can reproduce panels — techniques explained as we make repair sections for the Rapier's offside inner front wing.

Making A 'Pattern' Panel

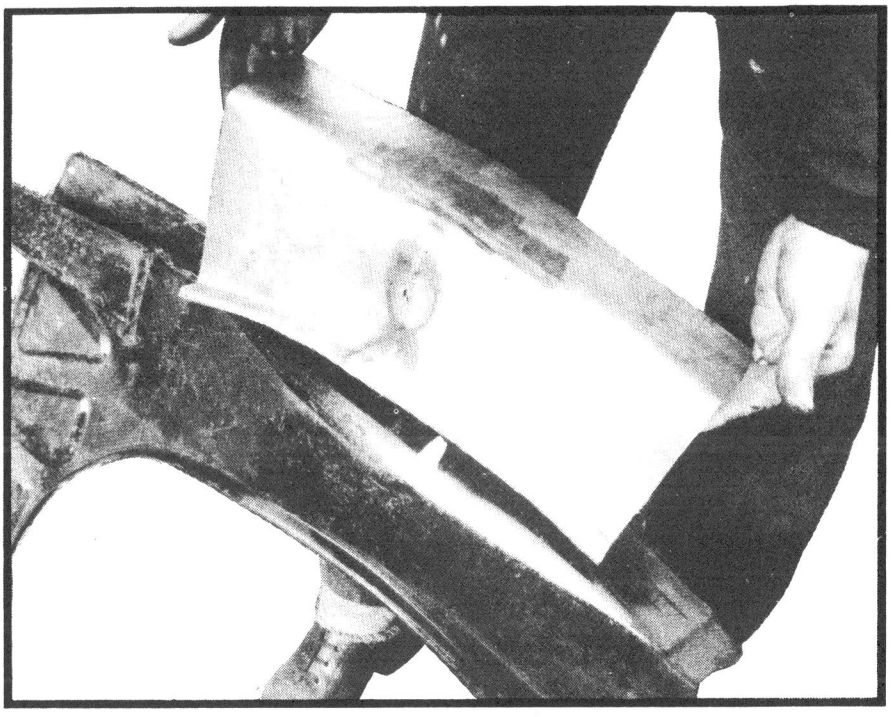

How to make a simple repair panel with the most basic tools; a technique demonstrated during the total rebuild of our 1960 Sunbeam Rapier

When by simple good fortune, we were able to purchase a pair of inner front wings for our Rapier, we knew that very few other owners involved in the restoration of Rapiers (or its Minx and Gazelle cousins which share the same bodyshell) could count on similar luck. So as we promised at the time, here's how you can fashion your own repair panels using only what's available in the average home-handyman's garage or workshop. And, of course, the basic techniques apply to the making of repair sections for any make of car.

First you need to produce a cardboard pattern of the section you want to make — and unless the section is almost flat, corrugated cardboard from a box isn't really suitable as it won't bent easily, so if you don't happen to have the right sort of material to hand, it's worth popping down to the stationers and buying a sheet or two of nice flexible card (preferably of a light shade so your markings show up clearly).

The procedures we're adopting here are not exactly those which a professional panel-man would use, but then he has facilities and skills which the average do-it-yourselfer doesn't possess. Also, we are really talking about making inner panels where if the shape isn't totally 'right', it won't matter because it isn't seen — so long as it fits correctly. However, with perseverance respectable outer repair sections can be made at home too.

Having established the area which needs to be replaced you will have to decide whether you can tackle making the new part in one or several parts and a great deal depends upon how complex the panel is and your metal-working skills. Most people tend to attempt too much in one go.

Offer up your cardboard and shape it round the existing, rusted, panel — which underlines what we often say about never destroying body structures before you've decided how you are going to replace them. If the panel curves in two directions, you may need to slit the cardboard and overlap it in order to follow the shape. Where two flat (or almost flat) areas are joined by a radius, like the Rapier's inner wing panel which bends almost at right-angles along its length, mark the area of the radius on the cardboard too as this will help you achieve the right degree of curvature when you come to shape the metal. Mark on the pattern any holes which will need to be reproduced.

Talking of holes, the Rapier's inner wing section has a large hole on the nearside where a captive nut locates the battery carrier. While the nut had rusted away from the old inner wing, the carrier itself still held it firmly in the correct position, so we could mark it on our cardboard pattern. A further small hole (on both sides) was for the headlight loom.

It is now a question of transferring the pattern to the sheet steel, and actually making the new panel. Do not be tempted to use very heavy gauge metal because it is difficult to work and quite often the shape of the panel and the way you have to work it will transform what starts as a flimsy sheet of metal into a strong, fairly rigid component. You can use steel cut from the roof or sides of a van or something similar but you will probably find new sheet steel easier to work with. The procedure is followed step by step in the pictures, and while a certain amount of trial-and-error is involved, basically it's a case of doing a bit at a time and constantly offering up the job to the car — so that if you make a mistake you can correct it almost at once.

Making A 'Pattern' Panel

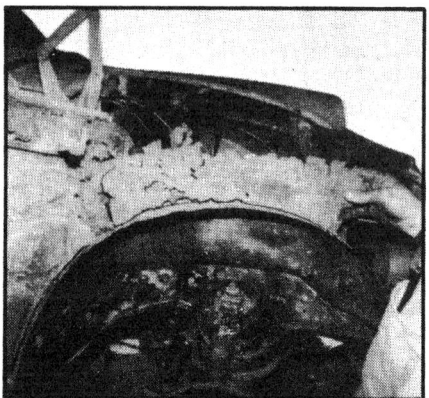

This is the section of inner wing needing replacement; either side of the piece Terry is holding the metal was sound, although is being removed because we are using complete new inner wing panels on our car.

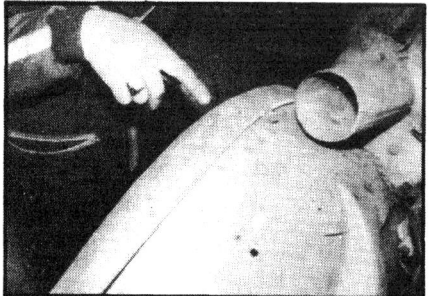

Curved part of wheelarch runs outwards at centre, and this must be accommodated in the 'pattern' part.

requires stretching the metal in the centre so that the ends of the panel begin to slope downwards. Also, the curved wheelarch section on the car widens out at the top, which means that the repair section also has to project outwards at this point, creating another dimension to be incorporated. A slit in the metal, with the overlapping piece cut out

Tools you will need

A good bench preferably with angle iron along one edge • A vice • Metal shears or alternative metal cutting equipment • Drill • Engineer's ball pein hammer • Panel hammer • An assortment of pieces of timber to assist in shaping • Gloves (leather) • Steel rule and set-square • Welding equipment.

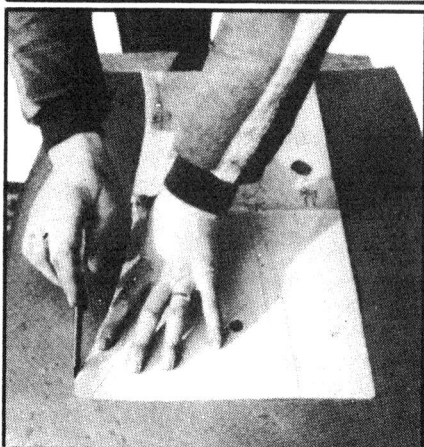

The cardboard pattern is laid out flat on a piece of 22 gauge steel and drawn round. A felt-tipped pen is best at this stage, being more visible than a scribed line and easier to follow corners accurately. Using the pattern upside down will give you the opposite-hand panel.

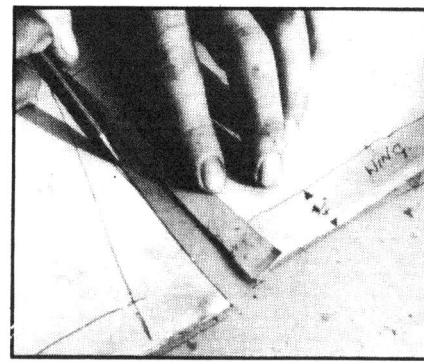

Here the 'V' section, which will later be cut out of the metal to allow the panel to assume the correct shape, is being marked, the cardboard having been cut and folded back here to allow the area to be marked out.

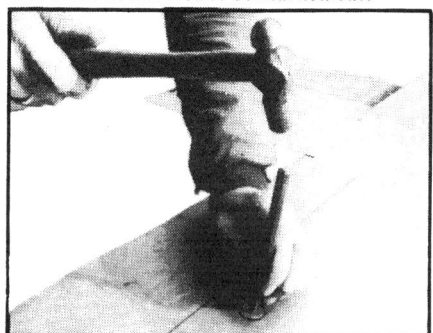

The holes are also marked, then centre-punched.

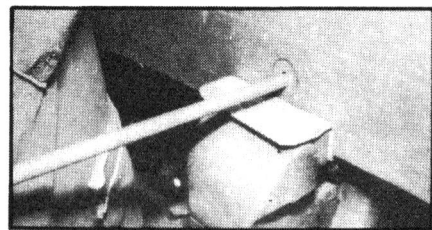

Each hole is drilled, then widened to the correct diameter with a round file — using successively larger ones as the hole gets bigger (if you have a selection). This job is easier done while the section is still a simple piece of flat steel.

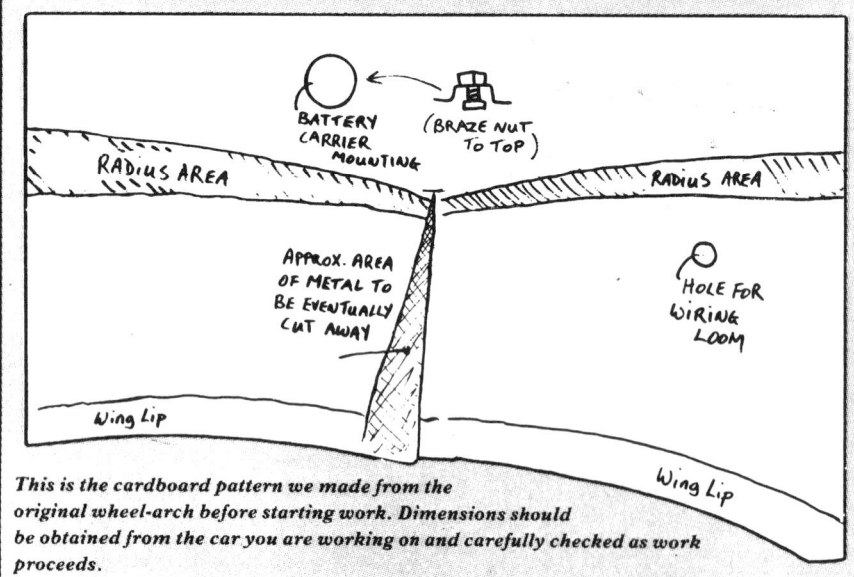

This is the cardboard pattern we made from the original wheel-arch before starting work. Dimensions should be obtained from the car you are working on and carefully checked as work proceeds.

The most difficult part in reproducing the Rapier/Minx inner wing section is getting the new section to follow the fore-to-aft curve of the original (where it meets the outer wing along the side of the engine bay), whilst also maintaining the curve from left to right. This double curvature is tricky to get right and

after the metal has been shaped, helps in this respect.

On our Rapier. the old outer and inner wings have both been removed because we have new replacements for them as mentioned. However, if you intend making up a new inner wing section as described, and will be

The basic shape is then cut out of the sheet steel, and also a single slit made (see line) where the 'V' cut-out will come.

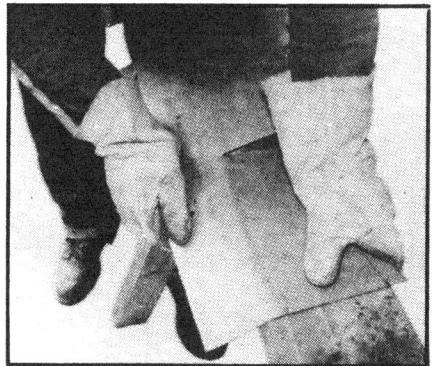

Using the radius location lines which you've drawn on the metal, gradually produce a gentle curve by carefully bending the metal over the edge of a bench, or suitably shaped length of wood or piping; flex the metal only very slightly each time, moving up and down between the guide lines so you don't get a right-angle or sharp creases.

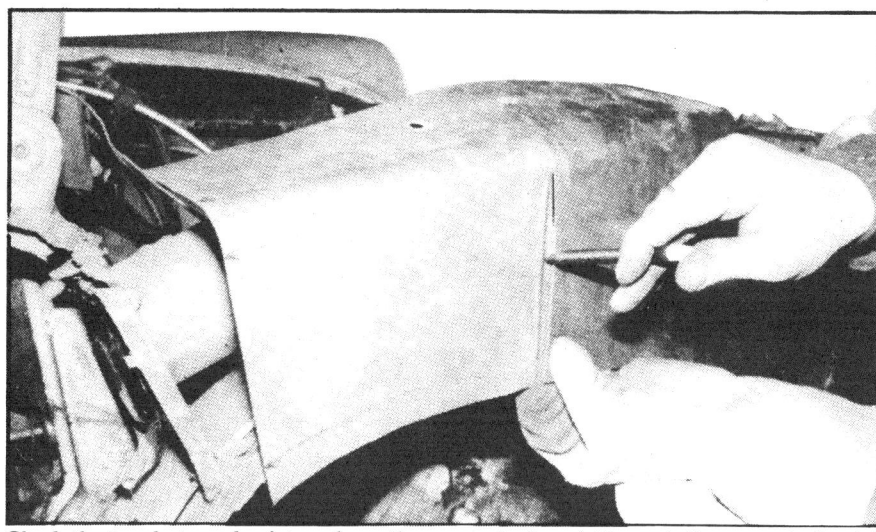

Check the panel at regular intervals on the car, and when right, mark the amount of metal which needs to be cut away due to the overlap brought about by the metal stretching.

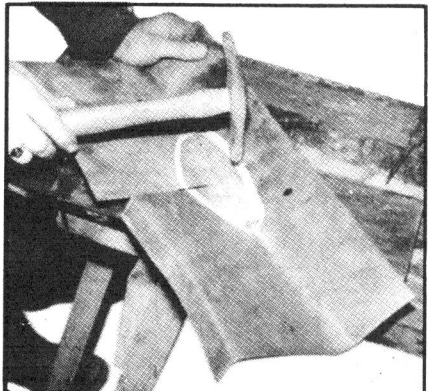

At the same time, dress the centre of the panel in the area shown to spread the metal in the middle, which will have the effect of making each end drop down. A length of timber with a hollowed-out depression in it is useful to assist this process. This process is being continued after one of the flanges has been made (see later).

The 'V' shaped slit of metal can then be cut away with shears.

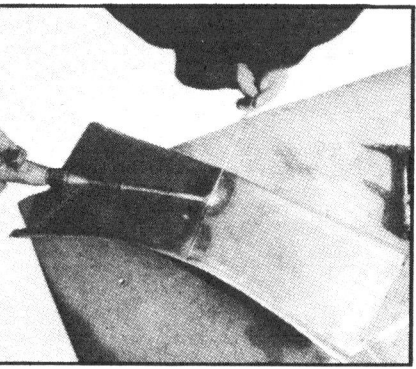

After a further check on the fit, the 'split' is brought together, clamped, and tack-welded top and bottom. It is the seam welded as shown here, the heat helping to pull the round to assist the top curve.

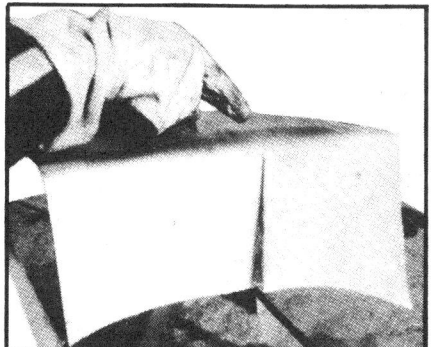

Eventually the metal will begin to overlap at the centre cut.

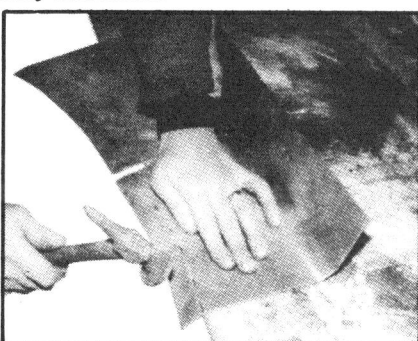

You can now tap out the right-angled bottom flange over the edge of a steel bench or piece of angle iron. Check against the car's wheelarch first to make sure the contour will be correct.

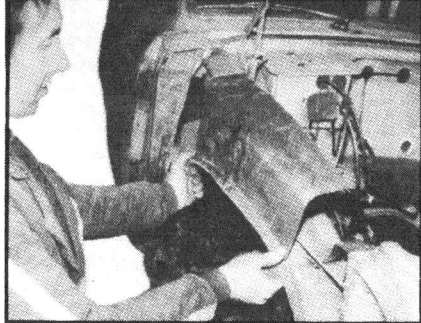

The finished repair panel in place; as mentioned, on Rapiers, Minxes and Gazelles of this period, this centre section is usually the only part which requires total replacement.

replacing the outer wing, make sure you leave the old outer wing flange in place (the one which runs either side of the engine bay) so that even if the inner wing has rotted completely away at this point, you will still have an inner reference point to work to when making your repair section.

The panel which is the subject of this feature isn't the simplest sort to make, so allow the best part of a day if you haven't tackled anything similar before; practicing the various

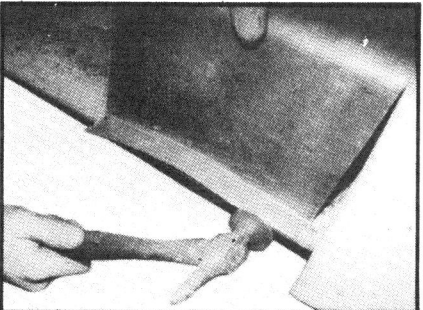

The small return lip can then be added to the flange in a similar manner, though using an old flywheel or similar will help you follow the radius.

techniques on scrap steel first may help you get the feel of working with metal. Later on, we will take the process a step further, and show how you can make much larger and more complex panels at home, including complete wings, if you're that ambitious. But next month, it's back to the Rapier rebuild again, as the bodyshell is very nearly finished now.

NEXT MONTH
Offside sill and wing replacement

Rapier Restoration!

Paul Skilleter concludes the story of the body repairs to our 1960 Series III Sunbeam Rapier.

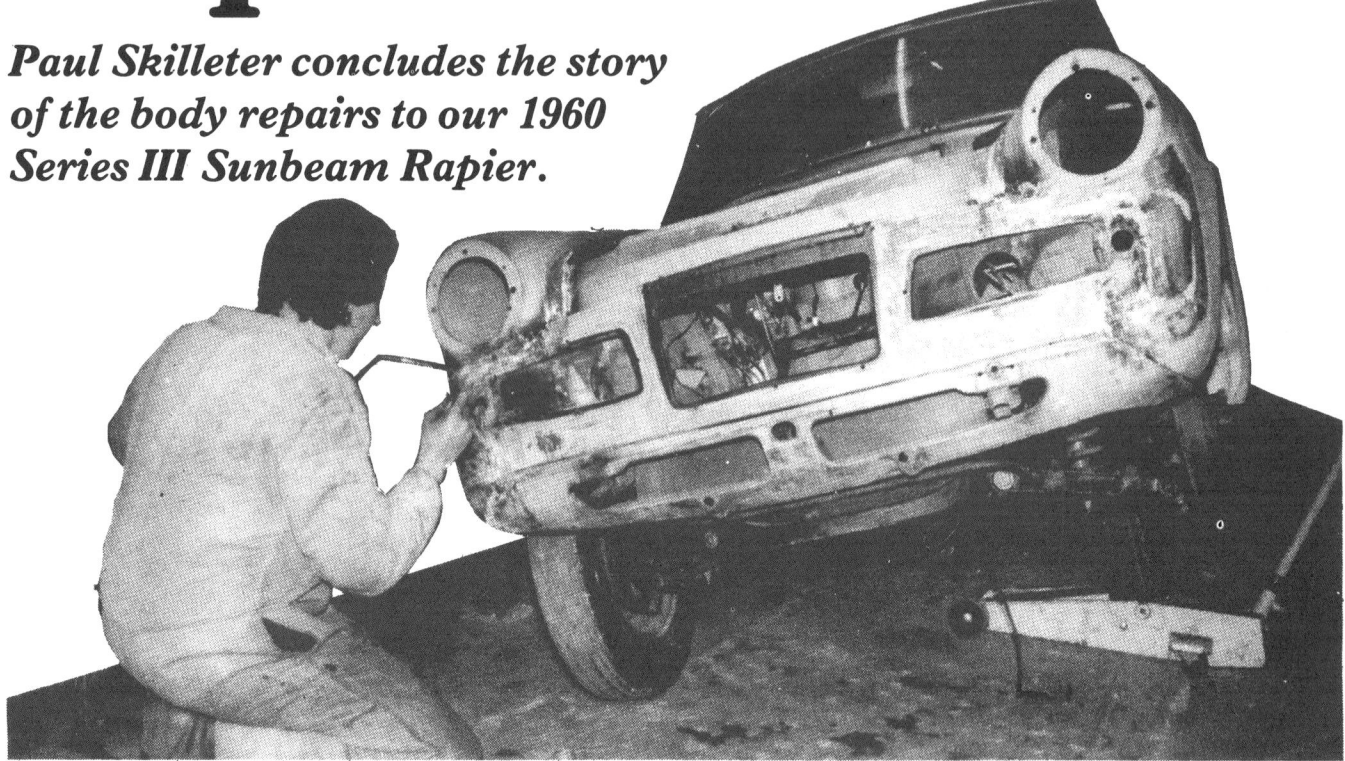

As you read this, Terry is putting the final touches to the Rapier's bodywork prior to taking it down to Cottons of Worcester for its repaint in grey and red, including lead-loading the alterations to the Hillman Minx front wings which we adapted, as shown in the heading picture. We have already covered the rebuild of the offside bodywork in some detail and, as the pictures show, the nearside work followed much the same lines.

To re-cap for the benefit of new readers, however, we found that the trickiest aspect of rebuilding this particular model was getting the sill line right. This is because the outer sill panel is far from being a straight run front to rear — it bows outwards, and also tucks in underneath just before it reaches the rear wheel arch area. As the only replacement sills we could find were pattern-type and a simple straight pressing, getting these various contours right demanded much trial fitting and gentle persuasion. Careful examination of

pictures and original cars also showed that the sill's top 'shoulder' is maintained all the way down the car right to the rear wheel arch — logically one might have expected it to be flush with the rear side panel behind the doors, but such a finish would definitely be wrong.

We were of course very much helped by the lucky chance of being offered new outer and inner front wings, although the former actually turned out to be Minx ones of the same period, which thus had to be adapted in the sidelight area. The inner wings were an even rarer find, which is why last month we outlined how to make repair sections for Rapier, Minx and Gazelle owners who are not fortunate enough to obtain these panels.

The last job before loading the car on the transporter was to go round and make sure that no rot had been missed (surprisingly easy to do, which is why a formal check a day or so before you are due at the paint shop is a very wise idea), and to seal all seams and overlaps. This both tidies up the job and prevents water from getting into metal 'sandwiches' and starting the rusting process all over again.

Nearside repairs needed mirrored those of the offside; here the new inner wing has been fitted, and Terry completes the patching of the bulkhead and footwell.

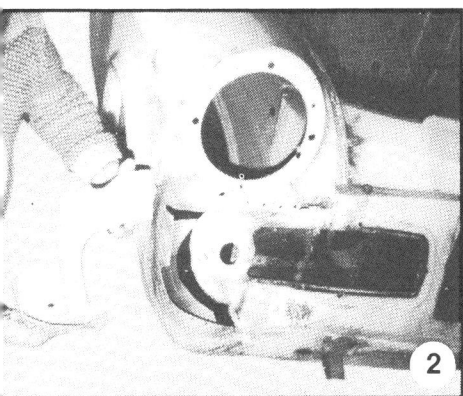

The new outer wing was trial fitted, and altered to Rapier spec. at the front — this is the Minx sidelight housing removed, showing the gap left to fill between wing and original front panel (around Rapier sidelight hole).

Outer sill has to be in place before the front wing can finally be installed. As we learnt from doing the same job on the offside, the sill (a 'pattern' one) has to curve quite sharply under at the rear, and curves from front to rear along the car.

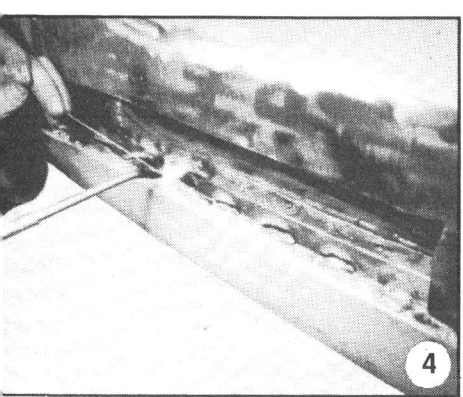

Here the outer sill is being welded to the box-section inner sill/chassis member extension, which has already been repaired.

This rear side area can only properly be repaired if the side panel is cut away at the bottom; here Terry offers up the replacement section he has made — note rebated edges which will result in an almost flush join with the original outer panel.

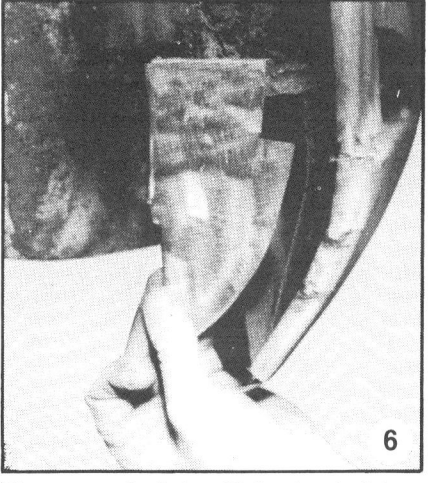

The rear end of the sill is closed-off by a made-up panel where the original wheel arch had rusted away. For those who missed previous episodes, this view shows the centre 'membrane' or middle sill wall which runs from front to rear down the car. The bottom half of this on both sides was replaced by an adapted MGB centre membrane, the nearest panel we could find to the original.

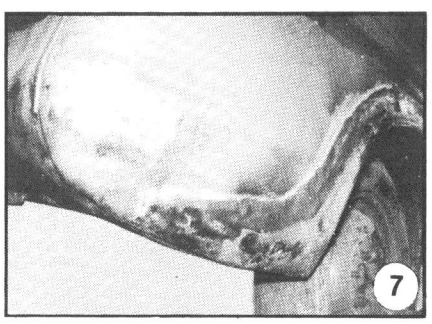

The rear wing lip was repaired from sections taken from the old front wing; the bottom of the wing was also badly damaged by rot and Terry had to make up sections shaped to fit the curves at this point. The inner skin behind also needed repair.

As on the offside, the nearside front footwell had holed in the corner and along part of the sill.

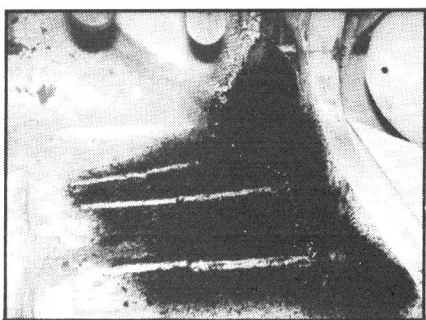

Repair of the footwell was not too difficult, although the curved section near the throttle pedal was tricky to shape. The area has been sprayed with under-sealant to match the original finish, and later will be sprayed body-colour.

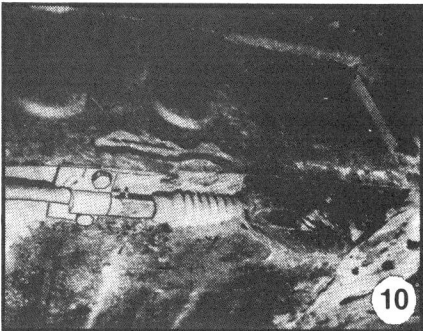

A bit more complex was the rot under and around the handbrake cable mounting bracket, on a plate secured by two bolts in captive nuts. These nuts are not accessible from inside the car as they are in the space between the floor and the channel-section plate.

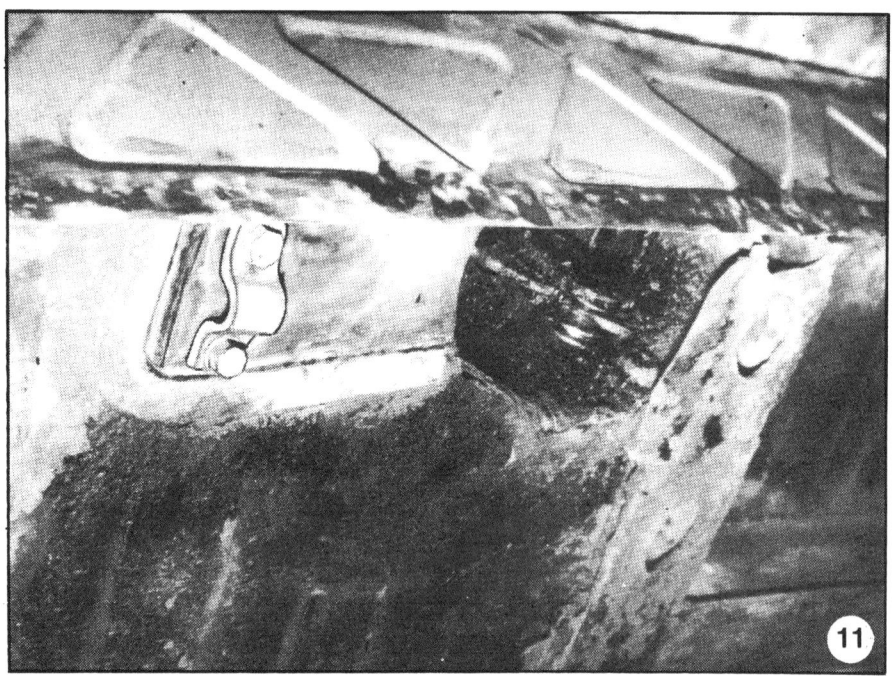

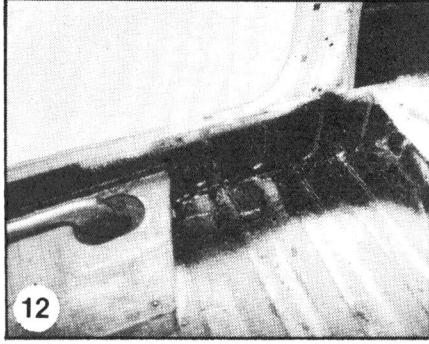

This is the same area from the top after the repairs to the floor above the plate have been finished.

The handbrake assembly had to be removed and a new plate made-up; new captive nuts were brazed into place using the original plate as a guide. Also visible is the MGB panel used to repair the centre membrane.

As the Rapier will see a period of active service as Assistant Ed John William's staff car, it is not going to be finished to near-concours standards as our Morris Minor was. Consequently, we are not painting the engine bay or preparing the underside to 'new' standards, as these would be impractical to maintain in that condition with the car in all-weather, everyday use.

Although the body rebuild has been successfully completed, there is lots more to come which should continue to interest Rapier and Minx owners, as when the car returns from Cottons we will be examining the suspension, steering and brakes in detail, bringing them up to scratch for the MoT test which will follow. So watch this space! ☐

As a guide for Cotton's painter, we are sending down the old front wings to show where the red stripe runs, as of course the new wings are simply primered. Note that wing lip has been removed to affect repairs to the rear wings.

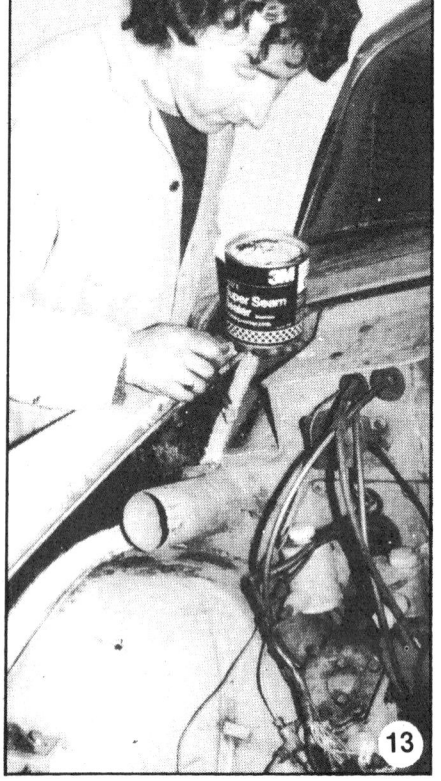

One of the final jobs before paint was to go all round the car sealing joints and overlaps with seam sealer. This is brushed on and into seams, and sets firmly but flexibly, stopping water getting between the metal and causing rust.

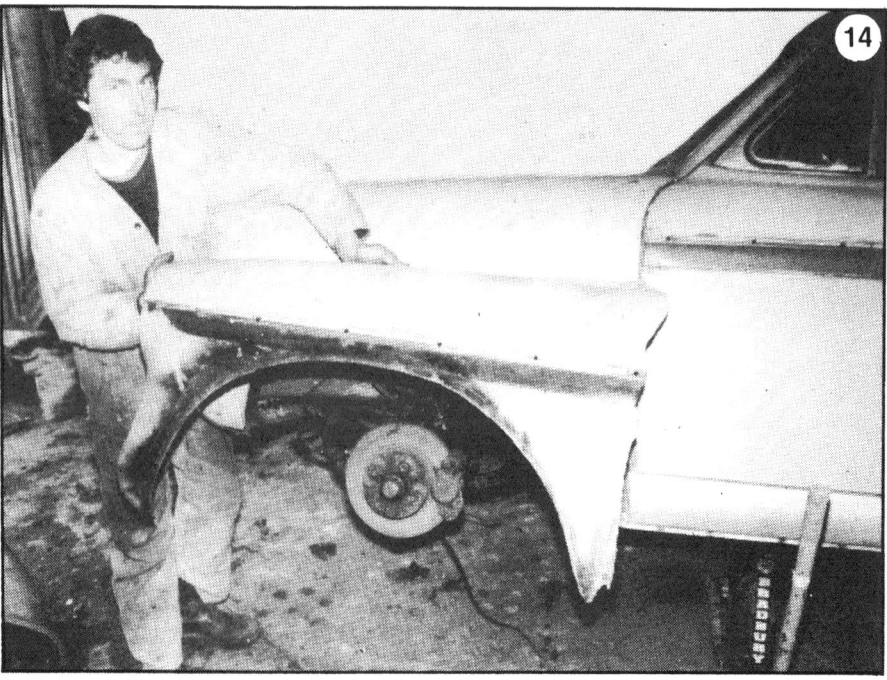

Rapier Restoration!

A look at the reassembly of our 1960 Mk III's engine, a job now in progress while the bodyshell is away being painted. Paul Skilleter reports.

The 1494cc power unit fitted to our Rapier was in its varying forms and capacities the mainstay of the Rootes range for many years, also being used in the Hillman Minx and Singer Gazelle and Vogue. It has the reputation for being a pretty tough unit too, capable of giving long service if reasonably well maintained, and with few inherent weak points. As regular readers will know, on strip-down our particular unit proved to be in very good all-round condition, despite emulsified oil caused by a leaking head gasket.

Both block and crank looked in excellent shape and after consultation with G.N. Richardson of Hartlebury we decided not to rebore or regrind. So the crank was merely polished, and the bores honed to remove the oil glaze. The standard pistons were near perfect with no signs of scuffing or blow-by, and just needed equipping with a new set of rings. New bearings were obtained, also in the standard size, while gasket sets, timing chain and tensioner, oil pump and other bits and pieces were ordered from the Rootes specialists R.J. Grimes of Hadleigh Garage, Marlpit Lane, Coulsdon, Surrey (01-668 1455/8) — who managed to supply everything on our shopping list for the engine overhaul with not a single default.

The photographs show the engine coming together, covering some of the important points to watch rather than being a complete step-by-step coverage of the operation. For detail advice, like us you can turn to the useful Haynes manual (this covers Rapiers and Alpines from 1955 to 1965, and Singers from 1958 to 1965), and the official Rootes workshop manual for the Rapier III to IV and Alpine I to IV which is still in print. You can obtain the latter from the Sunbeam Rapier Owners Club, incidentally, and is well worth acquiring if you have one of these cars.

Some general and specific points come to mind as worth emphasising. The first is cleanliness — every item used for reassembly must be spotlessly clean, and that means in all the ridges and crevices too, not just the big flat areas which are easy. Terry and I used a two-bath process, the first bath being to get the worst of the grime off, and the second used just before reassembly to remove the last particles of dirt; the cleaning fluid can be

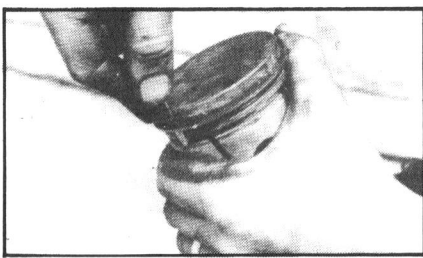

Having decided to re-use the original pistons, the old rings were removed by inserting a feeler gauge blade and running it round.

An old piston ring broken in two makes a good groove cleaner. If the break is not a clean right-angle one, use one of the ends. Afterwards, offer up correct 'old' ring to groove and check side clearance, which should be .0015 - .0035 ins for both compression and scraper rings.

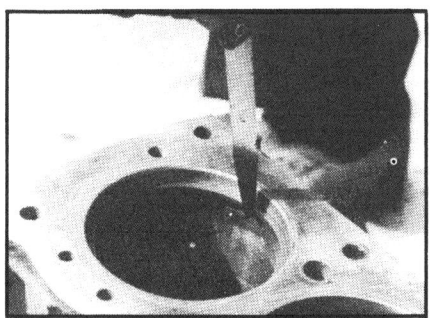

We fitted a new set of rings — in which case it's a very good idea to check them in the bore first, before trying to hammer a piston home! You can use a piston upside down to get the ring square in the bore before measuring the clearance; obviously push it down below any ridge.

petrol, paraffin or spraygun cleaner (we used Jetwash which smells like cellulose thinners and has a very searching action).

Some sort of airline is preferable to rags for drying, the latter being inclined to leave bits of fluff which could possibly build up and clog oilways. We found that the little compressor sold by Transpeed was good enough for the purpose, provided you let it build up pressure for a few seconds. But even a footpump will do for clearing oilways and crevices.

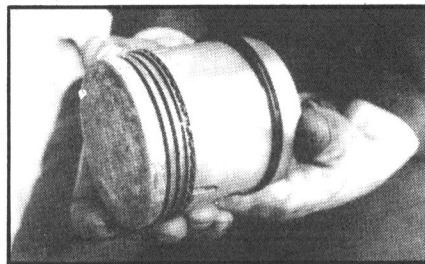

The new ring set (from Associated Engineering) came with this special type of Apex oil control ring. Always fit new rings according to the instructions as they are very easy to break or insert wrongly.

Rings can also be easily broken during the refitting of pistons to bores — the use of a good quality clamp is highly advisable.

The essential thing to remember when tapping the pistons home with wooden hammer handle or similar is to stop if any resistance is felt, then start again. Beforehand, as our block didn't need boring, the glaze had been removed; if this isn't done, the rings won't bed-in and you may get excessive oil consumption.

Being able to get away with simply re-ringing the pistons saved us a useful amount of money, but rings are still expensive and it pays to take care fitting them. Follow the directions which normally come with them, and note that when rings are supplied for an engine that hasn't been rebored, the top compression ring will have a step so that it doesn't hit whatever

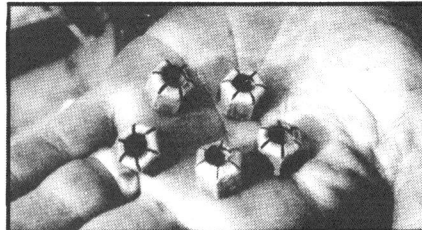

This engine has self-locking nuts securing the big-end caps, and are best renewed — certainly if they can be screwed on by hand.

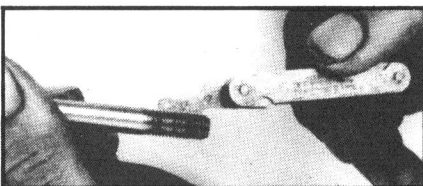

Watch out too for stretched bolts during bottom-end reassembly; a useful tool for checking on this is a thread gauge — select the correct gauge and if the bolt threads don't match all the way, use a new bolt.

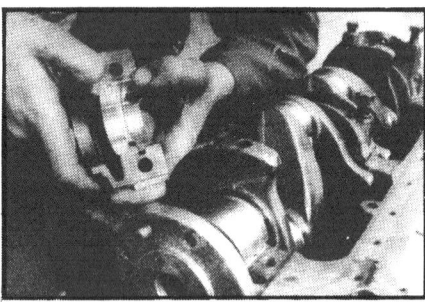

Crank was fitted into crankcase with the two (new) centre thrust washers installed correctly against side faces of the centre main bearing. New bearings were inserted in main bearing caps and fitted after being well oiled.

Bolts were then tightened to the correct torque setting of 24 lb/ft. The official manual warns against using 3/8 ins x 24 threads per inch nuts used on some other Rootes cars in place of 11/32nd ins — they will screw on but will strip at about half the correct torque.

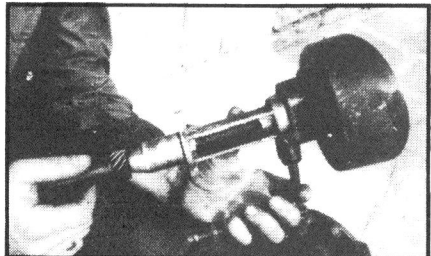

The Rapier's oil pump was dismantled and checked for wear.

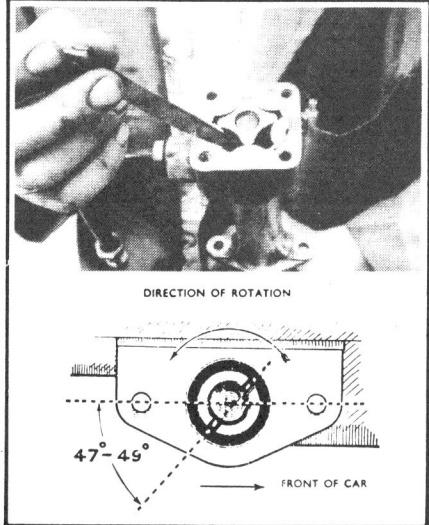

The clearance between lobes and inner rotor turned out to be .008 ins, or .002 ins more than permitted, so we fitted a new pump. Note that when replacing the oil pump, engine must be at TDC with piston of no. 1 cylinder in firing position as the pump must go back with distributor drive slot as shown in the diagram.

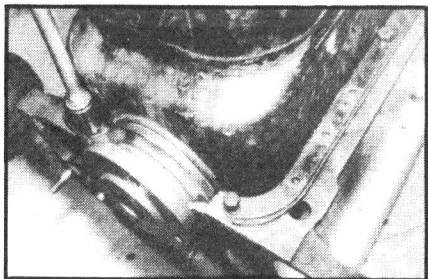

When refitting the sump, it's important to get an oil-tight seal at front and rear main bearing caps. This is best done by replacing front and rear securing bolts first, plus a couple at the middle of each side to locate the gasket, and tighten down. The official manual advocates the use of Wellseal or similar at ends of semi-circular cork (or rubber) seals.

ridge may be present at TDC (fit a non-stepped ring at the top by mistake and it'll probably break instantly). Obviously this ring must be fitted with the step upwards; usually rings will be marked 'top' in any case.

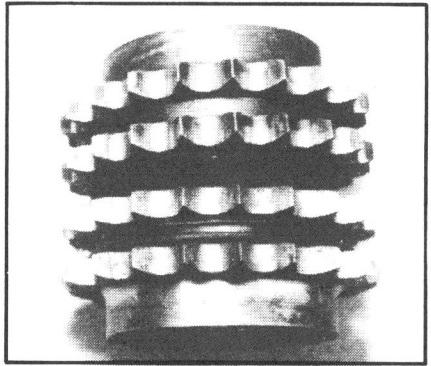

It's no good refitting worn timing wheels as they will ruin a new chain. Note that replacement wheel (bottom) has rubber tensioner between rows of teeth, which should make for quieter running.

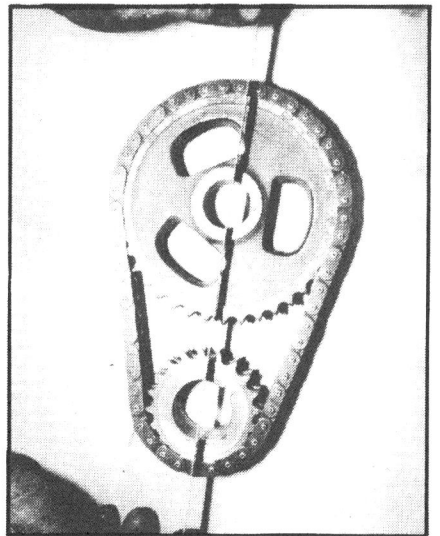

Timing wheels must be replaced so that the timing mark dots line up opposite each other where wheels are closest, and exactly on the centre-line through the wheels. This can be checked with a hacksaw blade used as a straight-edge.

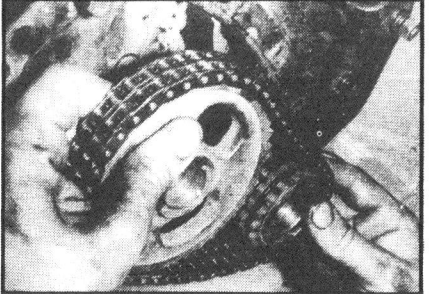

When offering up the assembly, no. 1 and 4 pistons should be at TDC, with the key to the top of the crankshaft. The camshaft is then turned so that its key lines up with that of the camshaft wheel. This should give you the correct valve timing. Next we fitted the crankshaft oil thrower, and a new chain tensioner.

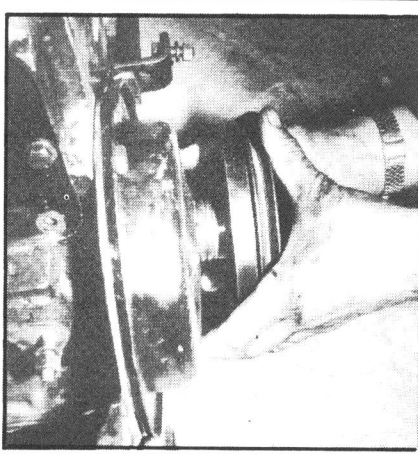

It's essential to centralise the timing cover around the crankshaft oil thrower before tightening the bolts, as any lack of clearance may result in a fireworks display when you try starting the engine. The manual advises use of a special tool, but one dodge to ensure clearance is to wind Sellotape round the thrower, removing it after you reckon to have sited the timing cover properly and tightened it down. Pulley itself is then offered up and driven into place, and secured with nut and locktab.

Engine side cover was bolted to block, head gasket placed in position, and the alloy head lowered onto block — having remembered to fit the rocker shaft oil feed pipe first.

Likewise, an oil drain ring must be fitted so that it directs the oil back into the sump and not into the combustion chamber!

When re-assembling virtually any component, make a last visual check for dirt then coat it with clean engine oil from a can (or from a Fairy Liquid bottle or similar). Take extra care with bearings, starting with a further last check to make certain that you have indeed been supplied with the correct size. We replaced all the bearings in our engine except those for the cam, which were in perfect condition. The cam is fitted before the oil pump is installed, by the way, on this engine. As mentioned in the picture captions, some wear was evident in our pump and so it was replaced by a new one.

The Rapier's alloy cylinder head was in excellent shape with guides, seats and valves all

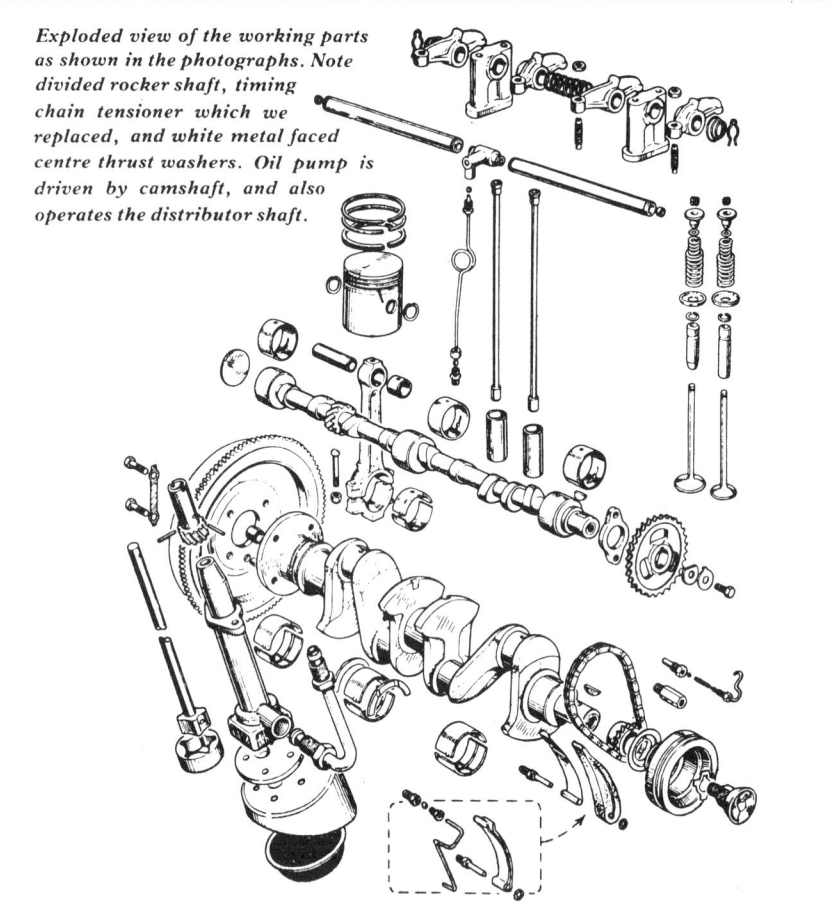

Exploded view of the working parts as shown in the photographs. Note divided rocker shaft, timing chain tensioner which we replaced, and white metal faced centre thrust washers. Oil pump is driven by camshaft, and also operates the distributor shaft.

Cam followers had already been replaced (some were pitted so we rooted round the bits box and assembled a better set), and with the head in place, the push rods were dropped into position.

Head bolts need torqueing down before rocker shaft assemblies are added, because you then can't get to them. Head was tightened down from the centre outwards as is the usual practice.

Rocker shaft on the Rootes engine comes in two halves joined by brass union which accepts oil feed pipe from block. When replacing the shafts, slip rockers individually over each pushrod, otherwise one might be forgotten and slip to one side as shown here — in which case it might get bent if you don't notice and tighten down the shaft.

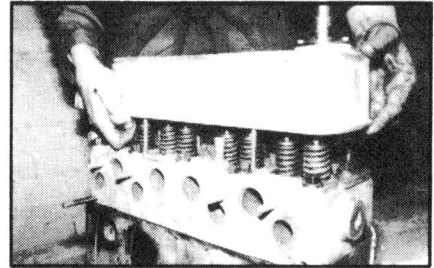

Finally the handsome cast aluminium rocker cover was fitted.

Checking the core plugs should be a routine procedure, and any that show signs of weeping or damage should be replaced. Many rebuilders replace them as a matter of course anyway.

in good condition, so it was just de-coked as normal and the valves ground-in. As a precautionary measure due to the fact that the car came to us with a blown head gasket, however, we had the head re-faced just to take care of any possible slight distortion or other irrgularity which could induce this fault to re-occur with the rebuilt engine. As little as possible was taken off the head though, as the existing compression ration of 9.2:1 is already on the high side for the 4-star fuel which is the best you can get today.

The engine is now nearly ready to go straight back in the car when it returns from the paintshop, though in the meantime we shall be undertaking some component overhauls. Then while the gearbox appeared to work perfectly, the overdrive unit didn't operate at all so that is also on our list for a check over. All to come in future instalments!

NEXT MONTH
Overhauling the Rapier's twin Zenith carbs and looking at the overdrive.

Overdrive Investigation

*We take a look at how overdrives work
— or don't as the case may be! — as we tackle
the one fitted to our Project Car Rapier.*

The Laycock overdrive is very definitely a part of the 'fifties/ 'sixties sporting scene; many cars with pretensions to performance (any many without too) came from the manufacturer with overdrive either standard or as an option, and a very worthwhile device it was too — or is still, because while it isn't seen as much as it used to be, it can still be specified on some new cars today.

The main purpose of an overdrive unit is to make available an extra, usually fifth, ratio which is considerably more highly geared than the normal top gear, the object being to provide unstressed, high-speed travel at low revs, aiding economy and the longevity of the power unit. It also gives the manufacturer the option of reducing the axle's final drive ratio, enhancing acceleration through the gears and in direct top — which is why the overdrive was popular on rally cars some twenty years ago when our Series III left the factory.

Having been able to drive our Rapier briefly before it was taken off the road for rebuilding, we knew that the overdrive didn't work. It would have been an advantage to have carried out various test procedures while the car was still mobile, so that any repairs could be verified on the road, but unfortunately time was lacking at that stage, so we were faced with the problem of diagnosis with the overdrive and gearbox detached from the car and lying on the bench.

With rare exceptions (the Jaguar XK 150S being one) the overdrive is controlled via a dash or gearstick mounted switch and a solenoid, the latter operating the lever which engages the overdrive. There are sometimes other circuits which effect the operation of the overdrive, such as a throttle switch which acts as a 'kick down' device and throws the overdrive out of engagement when the accelerator is pressed down sharply, a cut-out switch which prevents the unit being engaged when (say) first and second gears are being used, and/or a governor mechanism which does not allow the overdrive to be engaged below a certain speed (usually around 25-28 mph in top), due to there not being enough torque from the engine. Some overdrives are totally automatic, coming in as soon as top gear is engaged and the car reaches the speed mentioned, without there being any switch at the driver's disposal.

The overdrive has not, frankly, an unsullied reputation for being totally reliable, but many people have been deceived into thinking that some major expenditure is called for when only a minor electrical fault has occured — which is usually the reason for an overdrive unit packing up. This appears to be why the overdrive on our Rapier didn't work, though we cannot be totally certain until we get the car back on the road again in a few weeks' time.

Normally, the checks we carried out are done with the unit still attached to the car. We went straight to the solenoid itself as that's usually the culprit, and the easiest way to test this is to apply a current directly to it. The solenoid contains two coils, one heavy-duty winding which actually throws the overdrive engagement lever, and a second, lighter, winding which is automatically brought into operation at the end of the plunger's travel and which then holds the plunger in its extended position, using very little current. When testing the solenoid with a current taken directly from a battery, apply it only very briefly, just enough to see that the plunger works, otherwise you could burn out the primary winding.

As expected, nothing happened when we tested our solenoid directly in this manner, so we removed the unit for a closer look. The plunger simply pulls out of the body, and it looked somewhat decayed and could have been sticking. But the real cause seemed to be dirty points in the make-and-break contact set to be found inside the end cover, because a clean up of these with a points file immediately brought results. At first glance the solenoid looks like a sealed unit and no doubt many have been thrown away when they ceased to work, but

Overdrive Investigation

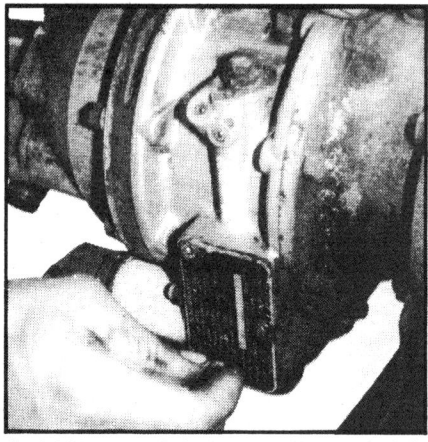

A sticking solenoid is the most likely culprit in a faulty overdrive. Plate gives access to plunger and operating lever.

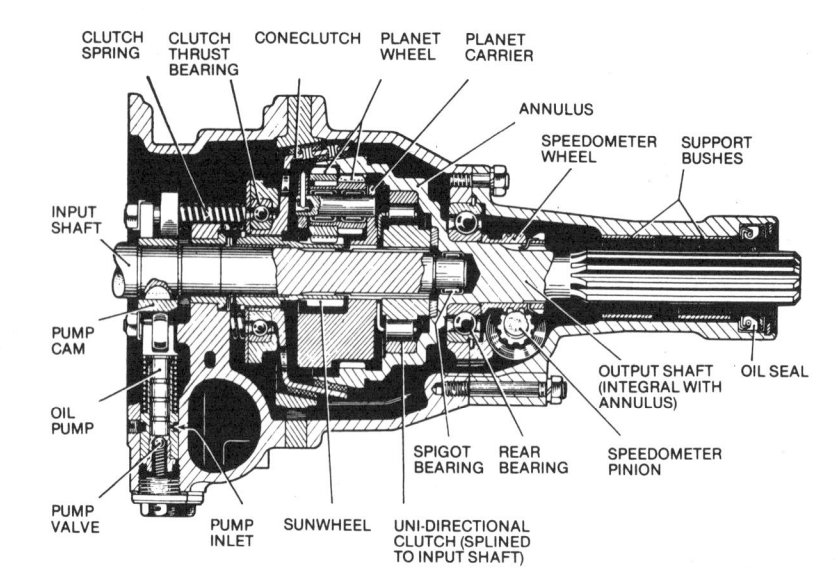

CLUTCH SPRING · CLUTCH THRUST BEARING · CONECLUTCH · PLANET WHEEL · PLANET CARRIER · ANNULUS · SPEEDOMETER WHEEL · SUPPORT BUSHES · INPUT SHAFT · PUMP CAM · OIL PUMP · PUMP VALVE · PUMP INLET · SUNWHEEL · UNI-DIRECTIONAL CLUTCH (SPLINED TO INPUT SHAFT) · SPIGOT BEARING · REAR BEARING · SPEEDOMETER PINION · OUTPUT SHAFT (INTEGRAL WITH ANNULUS) · OIL SEAL

Sectional view of the overdrive unit fitted to Rootes cars. It centres around a sun wheel and planet wheels; in overdrive the sun wheel is held stationary by the hydraulically operated cone clutch, and the planet wheels are driven round it thus rotating the tail shaft faster than the input shaft from the gearbox.

Here the plunger can be seen attached to operating arm, after the cover has been removed.

If you have removed the solenoid, it can be quickly tested by putting it across a battery — but only for a split second, enough to hear and see the plunger operate.

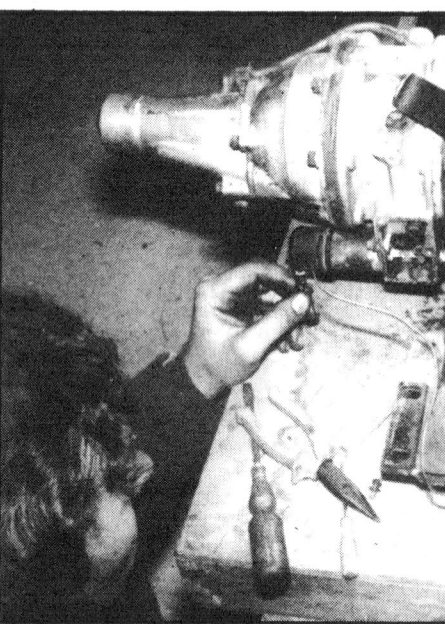

Replaced, the solenoid was again tested using a battery, earthed against the casing; a very brief touch of the lead against the terminal was all that was needed to show that the solenoid was operating the overdrive engagement lever.

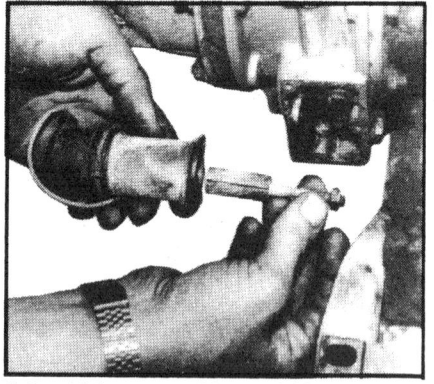

Solenoid is removed by undoing two small bolts holding the body, and the adjuster nut on plunger. Surface corrosion was evident on the plunger but this was probably from disuse, rather than being the direct cause of the unit not functioning.

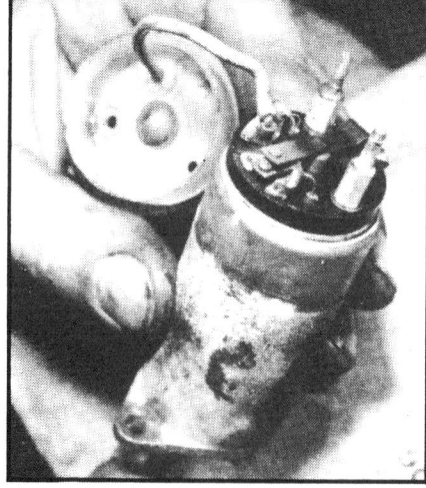

Under the end cap are points which close when the plunger moves forward to work the overdrive's operating lever and bring the secondary winding into play, holding the plunger forward. After cleaning these and the plunger, our solenoid apparently began at work normally.

elementary attention can often get them going again because they are in fact very simple with little to go wrong, so long as the windings haven't burnt out. However, having said that it is true that many overdrive faults can be traced to a weak or unreliable solenoid action, and if there is any doubt about whether you've

got it working properly, it is worth the relatively small expense involved in replacing it before considering the strip-down or replacement of the mechanical/hydraulic part of the overdrive.

If the overdrive had still been in the car, the next thing for us to have done would have been to take the car for a run to make sure that all was indeed okay. This would have shown up any further faults, such as poor connections (another common cause of overdrive malfunction), faulty relay, or faulty throttle switch (where fitted). To track these down

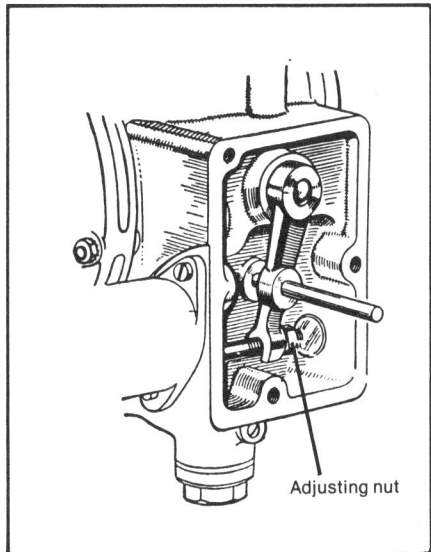

Careful adjustment is required to ensure that plunger is set correctly — if it is, a 3/16 ins diameter rod can be passed through the lever and into a hole in the overdrive casing with the ignition on, top gear engaged and the overdrive switch 'on'. A suitable drill bit can be used for this.

Adjusting nut

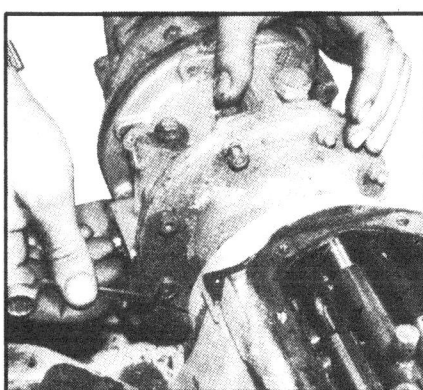

To remove overdrive from gearbox, just these nuts need be undone; the gearbox really needs to be taken out of the car first for this operation.

The overdrive can then carefully be withdrawn from the gearbox. Replacing it is more difficult as the two sets of splines inside the overdrive must be in line; normally a special tool is used but we offered the unit up to the gearbox, engaged the first set of splines, locked the gearbox and twisted the overdrive so that the second set clicked level with the first.

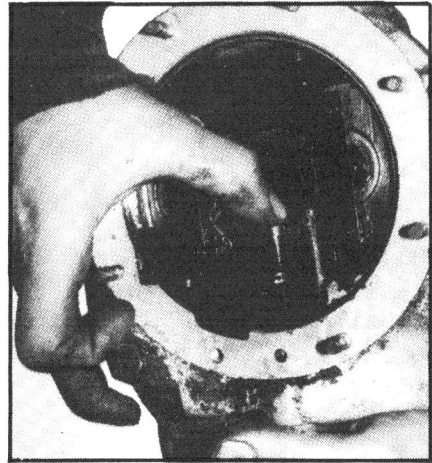

Cam on shaft works the oil pump inside the overdrive which provides the hydraulic pressure which operates the mechanisms. Cleanliness is vital when dealing with the internals of an overdrive, as any foreign matter, or even 'fluff' from rags, can effect the workings of valves etc.

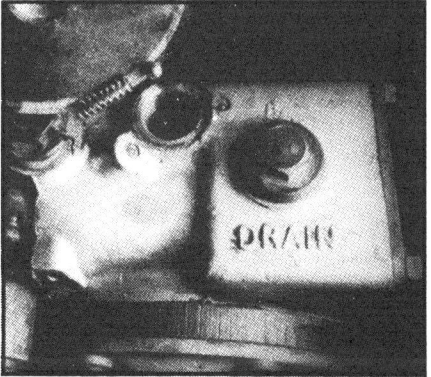

Relief valve can be checked by unscrewing wired plug on bottom of unit, having drained the oil first (we've replaced the drain plug to prevent dirt getting in). Spring and ball from relief valve can be seen here, held by magnet. If the ball doesn't seat properly due to dirt, the hydraulic circuits will be affected. Note: it is essential that pressure is relieved before commencing any dismantling, by operating the overdrive with the ignition on and the engine switched off some ten or twelve times.

Diagnosis of Faults
Taken from the contemporary Rootes Service Manual.

When positioning the vehicle for the removal of the Overdrive, care must be taken that the vehicle is *not* brought to a halt by stalling in gear.

When transmitting torque in forward direct drive, the rollers of the unit directional clutch are forced towards the crest of the facets of the inner member, and if the vehicle is brought to a halt by stalling in gear, the rollers can lock in the drive position, thereby preventing the removal of the Overdrive unit.

If the overdrive unit does not operate properly, it is advisable first to check the level of oil and, if low, to top up with fresh oil and test the unit again before making any further investigations.

Before commencing any dismantling operations it is imperative that the overdrive switch is operated ten to twelve times with the engine stopped, ignition switched on and top gear engaged, to release any hydraulic pressure from the system. Faulty units should be checked for defects in the order listed below:

Overdrive does not engage
1. Insufficient oil in the gearbox.
2. Solenoid not operating due to fault in electrical system.
3. Control mechanism out of adjustment.
4. Insufficient hydraulic pressure due to leaks or faulty relief valve — Test pressure.
5. Leaking operating valve due to foreign matter on ball seat or broken valve spring.
6. Leaking pump non-return valve due to foreign matter on ball seat or broken valve spring.
7. Pump not working due to choked filter.
8. Damaged gears, bearings or shifting parts within the unit requiring removal and inspection of the assembly.

Overdrive does not release
IMPORTANT — This calls for immediate attention. Do not reverse car, as selection of reverse in overdrive can cause extensive damage.
1. Control mechanism out of adjustment or fault in electrical circuit.
2. Blocked restrictor jet in valve.
3. Sticking clutch.
4. Damaged parts within the unit necessitating removal and inspection of the assembly.

Clutch slip in overdrive
1. Insufficient oil in gearbox.
2. Control mechanism out of adjustment.
3. Insufficient hydraulic pressure due to leaks, or foreign matter in valves.
4. Worn or carbonised clutch lining.

Clutch slip in reverse or freewheel condition on overrun
1. Control mechanism out of adjustment.
2. Blocked restrictor jet in valve.
3. Worn or carbonised clutch linings.
4. Insufficient pressure on clutch due to broken clutch springs.

Hydraulic knock
This knock occurs once per mainshaft revolution in direct drive and can be eliminated by relieving the hydraulic pressure in the direct drive position by scoring the operating valve ball seat in the casing.

Overdrive Investigation

means using a test lamp and checking out the various circuits involved.

Less likely, but still possible, is some malfunction of the overdrive hydraulics or mechanics. The first thing to check here is the oil level; normally this is common to that of the gearbox, and a low oil level is often the cause of overdrive problems, especially clutch slip in the unit, or even total refusal to function. The second point to check on the hydraulics is the relief valve, because if foreign matter prevents the ball (or plunger on other versions) from seating properly, a loss of pressure will occur. Mechanically, the most likely fault if the overdrive doesn't appear to

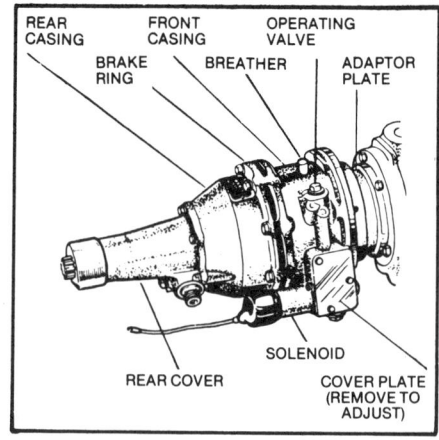

Sketch of the overdrive unit as fitted to the Rapier, showing the main external layout.

engage is worn-out clutch cone material, which is replaceable though somewhat expensive.

However, a strip-down of the overdrive unit is rather beyond the scope of this particular feature, though it's certainly something we intend to cover in the future. The aforegoing check points should satisfactorily take care of probably 90% of overdrive faults and the chances are you won't ever need to dismantle the entire unit.

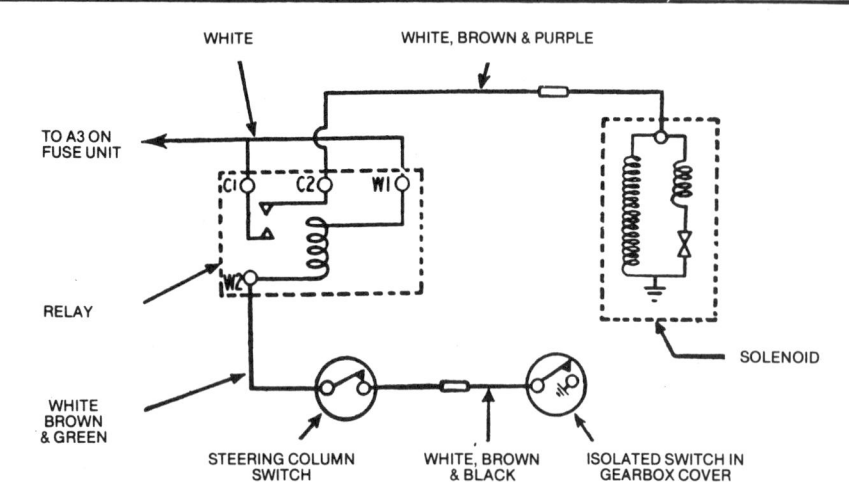

This is the basic overdrive wiring circuit for early Rapiers; note isolator switch on gearbox cover (which prevents overdrive working on 1st, 2nd and reverse), which should be checked with test lamp.

NEXT MONTH
Installing the Rapier's engine and gearbox

"*Looks like someone got here first…*"

Rapier Restoration!

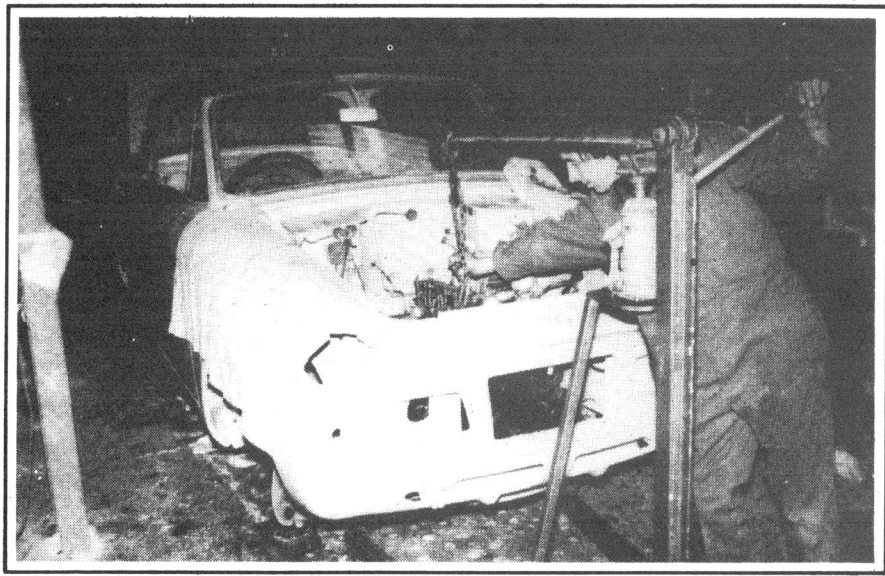

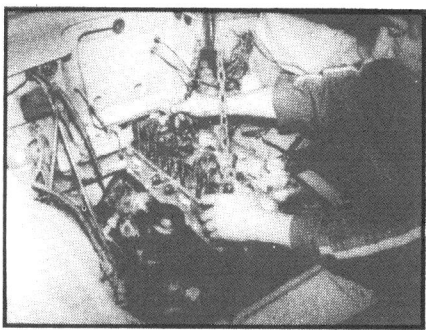

Gearbox is replaced first, then engine, which is lowered into bay and held level so that spigot shaft lines up correctly.

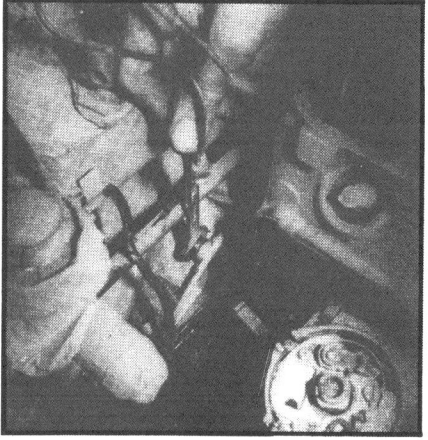

Bellhousing bolts are inserted and tightened.

Engine and gearbox go back in as our Sunbeam Rapier nears completion. Paul Skilleter brings you the latest.

Collecting the Rapier from the paintshop, we were pleasantly surprised at the attractiveness of the Pippin red and grey colour scheme — the dullness of the original paint certainly hadn't done it justice previously. But we didn't spend too much time standing in the sun admiring it, as the car is bound for a spell of duty as staff transport and needed to be made road-worthy as soon as possible.

The engine and gearbox had received attention as described in earlier episodes, the box needing little more than a change of oil although the engine required a complete overhaul. Incidentally, we ended up borrowing the correct tool when reassembling the engine to ensure that the timing cover was replaced with the correct clearance around the oil thrower — a critical point as the thrower can revolve against the cover if it's not right. Luckily we found a local ex-Rootes garage with the tool.

Replacing the engine in the car means putting the gearbox/overdrive unit back first, after detaching the prop-shaft from the back axle. The engine was then lowered into the car; the job was made a little awkward by the necessity to get it completely level in order to engage the spigot shaft correctly. Engine mountings were fitted to the power unit first and lined up after the engine had been mated to the bell housing. Something else done before the engine went in was to run a brass nut up the exhaust manifold down-pipe studs to ensure that the threads were free, to save hassle later — there isn't much space that side of the engine.

The twin Zenith carburettors had already been overhauled (they weren't in too bad a condition anyway) and will shortly be replaced so that the engine can be run; the original fan blade had cracked so we need to locate a new (or better) one but otherwise the power unit should be ready to go.

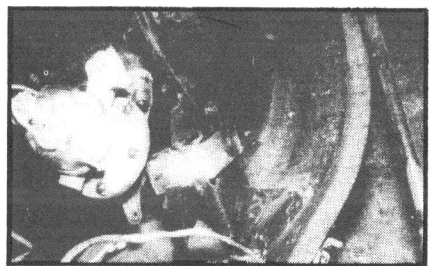

Weight of engine and gearbox assembly is taken by hoist, and the front engine mountings (which have been attached, complete with brackets, to engine beforehand) positioned on sub-frame by moving unit about until bolt holes line up.

Another job was to check over the suspension, steering and brakes. On the latter, we are renewing most parts as a matter of course because the car has an unknown history and has been standing for a considerable period. We shall be following most of that work in the next issue, when we will cover the re-piping of the car using a Handy brake pipe kit. ☐

NEXT MONTH
Overhauling the brakes and checking the suspension.

Rapier Restoration!

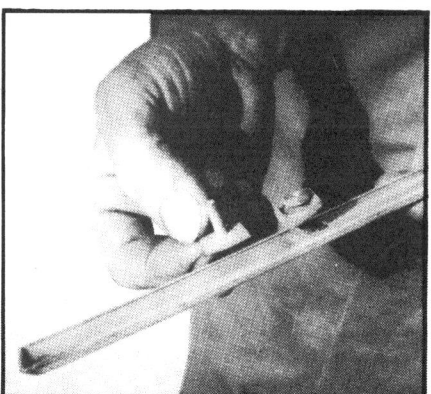

There's quite a lot of chrome bits and pieces to go back onto a stripped Rapier, and they use a variety of clips — simple ones which consist of just a plate with a screw through the middle (left) or more complex with plate fixed to stud, secured by nut, washer and rubber spacer on reverse side of panel.

Brake and suspension check-over as we prepare our 1960 Series III Rapier for the MoT. More news from Paul Skilleter.

By the time you read this, the Rapier should have been taken over by assistant ed. John Williams and be serving as an everyday staff car on the *Practical Classics* fleet. However, writing this at the beginning of September we are still in the midst of all the detail fitting-up and checking-over that always seems to drag on towards the end of a rebuild.

Many a would-be restorer has found that this stage is often the longest of all, having been under the delusion that getting the shell repaired and painted means that the hardest part is over; not so — putting everything back, and making sure every component functions properly beforehand, can take weeks and even months. And if you want to end up with a really good car, attention to detail and avoiding the temptation to hurry and get the car back on the road is essential, as we've often said before.

There's quite a lot of brightware on the Rapier and this had to be replaced, as shown in the pictures. Most of it is made from stainless steel and we were able to use the original items, supplemented by a few new pieces from the club or Grimes of Coulsdon.

Exceptions were the dummy front air intakes either side of the radiator grille, which (unusually) were not castings but were made of steel, which had rusted badly. A new offside grille was found but we've had no luck so far with the nearside one.

We were also supplied with a new radiator grille itself by Grimes, and noted that the replacement had aluminium anodised slats instead of the chrome finish of the original — obviously a later, cheaper, method adopted by Rootes. One important point to bear in mind on dismantling brightware is to keep track of all clips and fittings, as you may not be able to get satisfactory replacements; little items like these are all too easy to lose or throw away even, but can delay the finishing of a car by weeks.

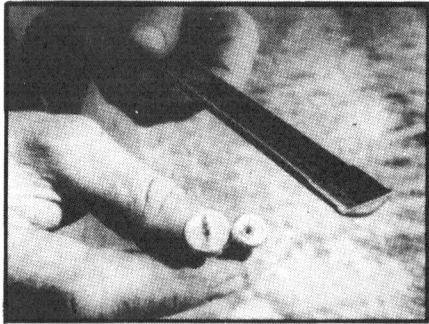

Mocern-type fixings are much quicker and easier to use, incorporating a Pop rivet — the round portion remaining a little proud of the bodywork to take the bright trim. However, the stainless steel strips on the Rapier were too stiff to be sprung over those clips in most cases, and we had to salvage the old types.

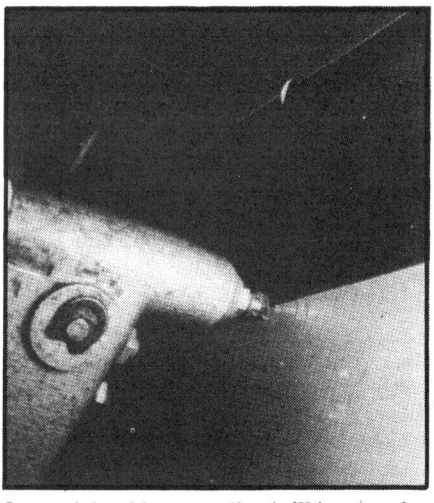

Some of the older-type clips (still in use today on occasion) are also Pop-rivetted in place, as shown here where the lower side body moulding fits.

tion! Rapier Restoration! Rapier Restoration! Rapi

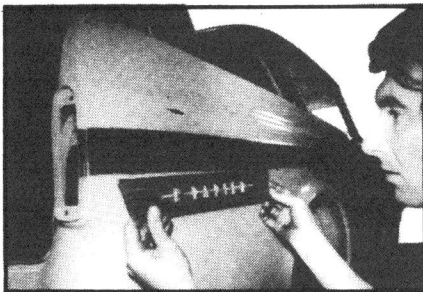

The 'Rapier' badge towards the rear fits on a separate, removable plate the purpose of which is to cover the spot-welded join where the Rapier fin assembly is attached to the basic Minx rear wing pressing which the car uses.

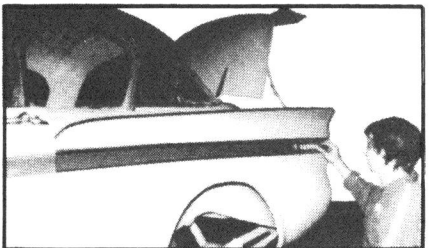

The similar name-plate on the other side slots into place; fin and body side mouldings have also been fitted up.

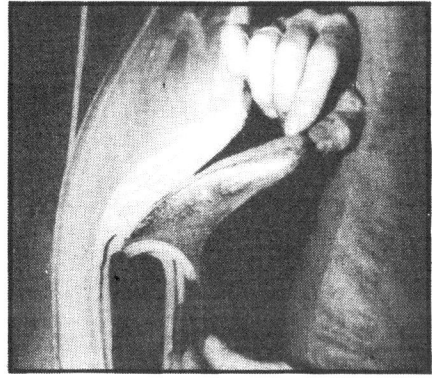

Mouldings are a mixture of originals and new obtained from the Sunbeam Rapier OC and Grimes, though we would like to locate a better offside fin capping as ours is decidedly beaten-up.

On the mechanical side, most of the brake hydraulics have been replaced, again by courtesy of Grimes, although the master cylinder was left as it appears good. Age and disuse had taken its toll of the front brake pistons and rear wheel cylinders however, and these have been renewed. Our apologies for not covering the re-piping of the system in this issue, but we just don't have the space this month. The full procedure will be relayed in an issue in the near future though.

Our Rapier had every sign of being a well-maintained car despite its rust (yes, we've tried to contact the previous owner but no success yet), so we weren't that surprised when we

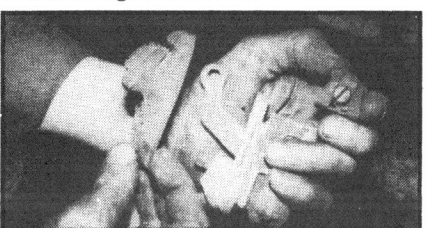

There doesn't seem to be a shortage of offside dummy grilles (we bought a new one from Grimes) but nearside ones appear completely unobtainable; so it looks as if we shall have to attempt a repair to our original, replacing the rusted-through bottom slat.

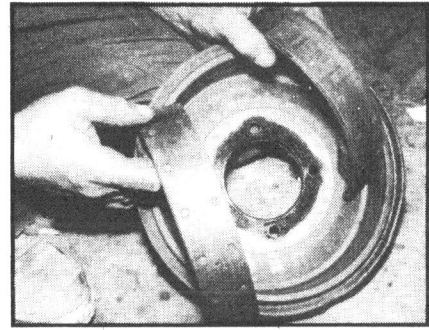

Rear brake cylinder incorporates the hand-brake mechanism and is very similar to the Morris Minor in this respect. And like a Minor too, the assembly had seized and has been replaced by a new one from Grimes. Adjuster is Minor pattern too.

Offside rear axle oil seal had failed, resulting in oil-soaked drum and linings, which will be replaced.

This entailed removing the half-shaft complete with back plate, oil seal and hub assembly.

The assembly was then taken to an engineering shop for the hub bearing to be pulled off the axle shaft — lucky we didn't try and do it ourselves because it took 20 tons pressure to shift it. Hub nut was rather chewed in the process so a new one was obtained. This picture shows the new seal in place ready for going back on the car.

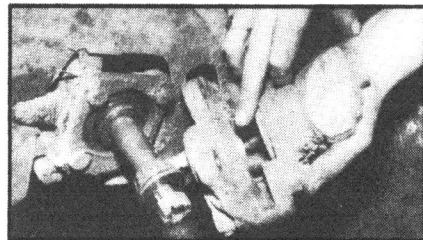

Front discs have been removed for skimming (they are well within the tolerance for this). Worn pads have meant that the wheel cylinders have been exposed to the elements and appear rusty, so may have to be replaced. Wheel bearings showed some play before the hub was dismantled and are being replaced all round, a sensible precaution at this stage of a rebuild anyway.

Here the new disc on the nearside suspension is being replaced after skimming.

Front suspension was checked for wear by lifting stub axle and feeling for play.

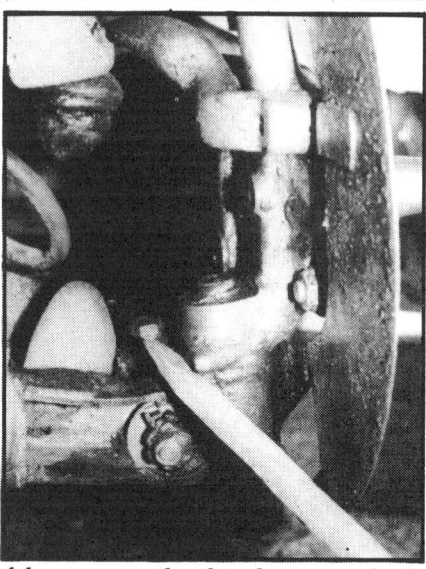

A lever was employed to detect wear in the lower trunnion, using it to lift the stub-axle assembly.

Gaiters were checked for splits, which allow dirt in and are an MoT 'fail' point. On our Rapier the front suspension and steering showed no detectable wear.

found no play or wear in the front suspension or steering, and no split dust gaiters anywhere. We paid particular attention to the steering joint located on the nearside of the engine bay as this is very difficult to dismantle with the engine in place, but like the remainder of the steering it was in good order. In some ways all this good news was welcome, but on the other hand we would like to have shown the over-haul of the Rootes suspension and steering; possibly we will return to the subject after the car's tour of duty.

NEXT MONTH
Re-piping the brakes, and more fitting-up.

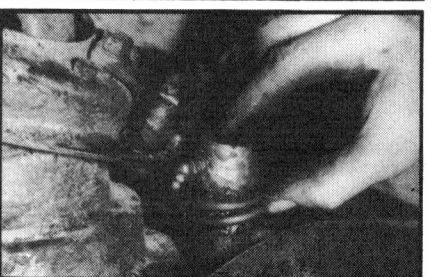

Our Sunbeam Rapier being fitted out with a complete set of Handy Brake Pipes. The car will soon become the everyday transport of our assistant editor John Williams.

Brake Line Replacement

Of all the causes of brake failure, rusted-through brake pipes must be the most common — and this can occur on cars only four or five years old. So it is a very good practice to examine your car's entire braking circuit at least once a year in order to spot the effects of corrosion, paying special attention to those lengths of pipe which accumulate mud or are subjected to constant bombardment from the road wheels.

At the very minimum, any dodgy-looking lengths of pipe should be replaced at once, but as internal rusting can also take place, on an older car it can be a wise move to install a totally new set — which gives you complete peace of mind at not very much cost (around £14-£30 for the average car). And while you're doing that, you might just as well use a completely non-rusting pipe and thus solve the problem of corrosion for good. This was certainly our train of thought as the job came up on our Sunbeam Rapier, which is about to face the rigours of a salty British winter, and so on went a 'Handy' brake pipe kit.

First step, after getting the car safely off the ground at one or both ends, is to apply the wire brush and (if necessary) degreasing fluid to clean all the unions and other brake parts you will be working on. This makes things more pleasant and prevents dirt getting where it shouldn't during the course of the job. Brake

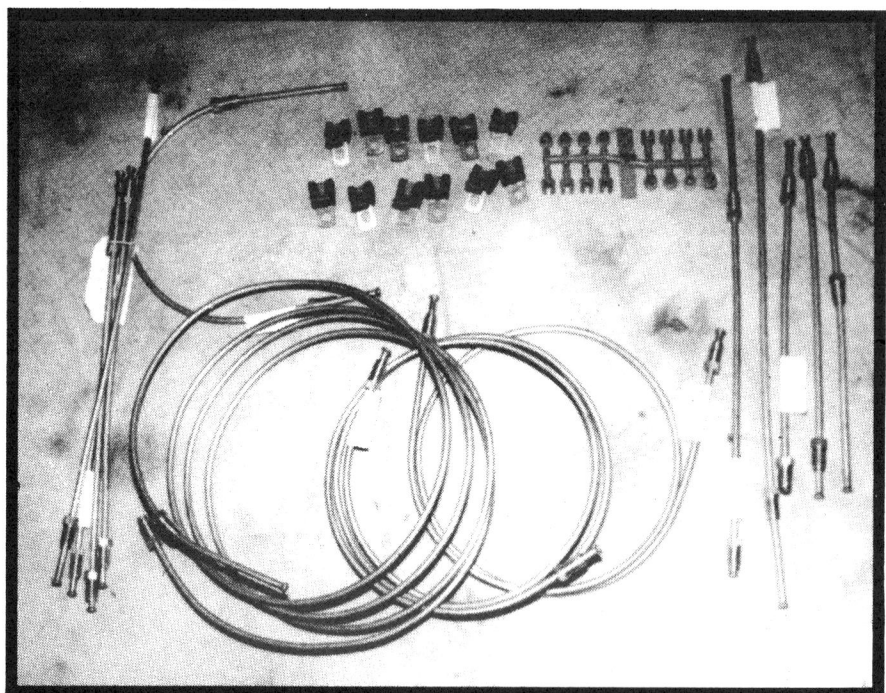

The brake pipe kit as supplied by Handy, complete with clips and with all pipes labelled; longer lengths are coiled.

The condition of your car's metal brake pipes is a vital safety point. Here we cover the installation of a Handy brake pipe kit on our 1960 Sunbeam Rapier.

drums should come off, and wheel cylinders inspected for leaks and seizure as this is a good time to tackle these too.

If you are intending to replace only the rear brake lines, in the vinicity of the rear axle, you can obtain a special clamp which squeezes the flexible pipe leading to the axle and prevents the rest of the circuit from ingesting air. If, like us however, you are replacing the entire system this isn't needed, and where you start dismantling isn't critical. Anyway, if you don't know when it was last replaced it's best to throw away the old brake fluid altogether, as it's bound to have absorbed a good deal of moisture over the years, which will affect the master and wheel cylinders even if it can't harm the Handy copper tubing.

The chances are that during dismantling at least one connector nut will refuse to come undone using a normal open-ended spanner, and the best advice here is not to waste time but simply cut through the old pipe and then use a ring spanner on it. Take a good look at the flexibles too, especially near their ends — bend them over and look for cracks. If in doubt, replace — they can expand internally with age and cut down the pressure to the wheel cylinders.

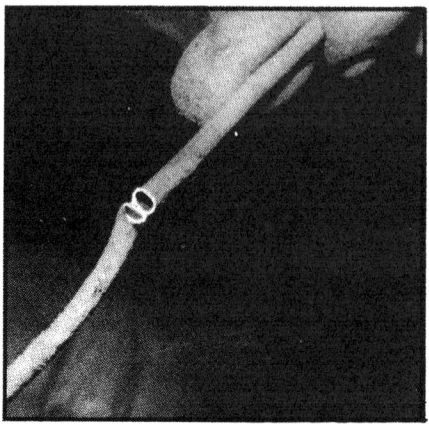

Old mild steel brake pipes can be lethal — this one broke after just a couple of bends.

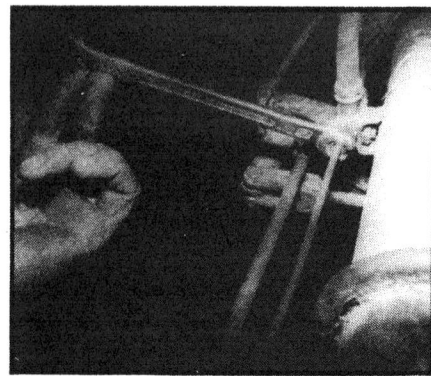

This brake spanner is a useful tool — it's like a ring spanner but with a slot cut out, and it allows a much better grip on the brake nut than an open ended spanner.

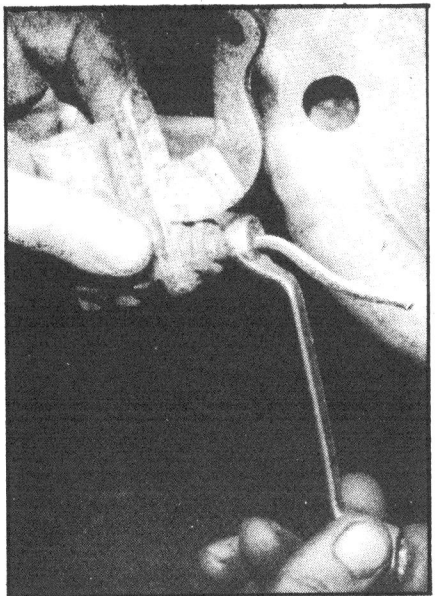

If a nut just won't undo, cut the old brake pipe which will enable you to bring a ring spanner to bear.

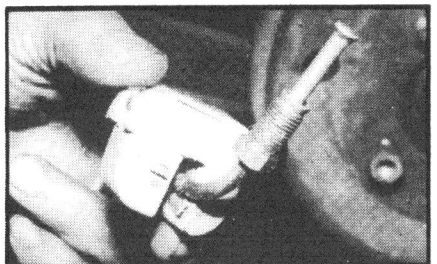

A junior hacksaw is ideal for cutting through old brake pipes, although professionals sometimes use this little device which can operate in a very restricted area — its cutting wheels are adjusted onto the pipe and the tool is then revolved. Useful for petrol lines too and it leaves a non-burred end.

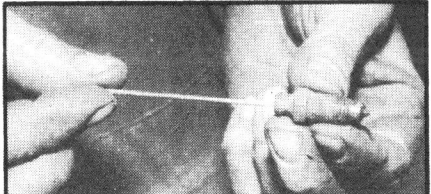

Don't forget to remove and thoroughly clean all bleed nipples with a bit of wire (or replace them with new ones). They often become blocked and this is a good opportunity to service them.

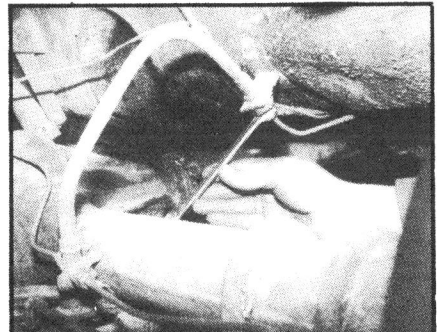

Here the fore-to-aft brake pipe is being disconnected from the flexible which connects to the back axle.

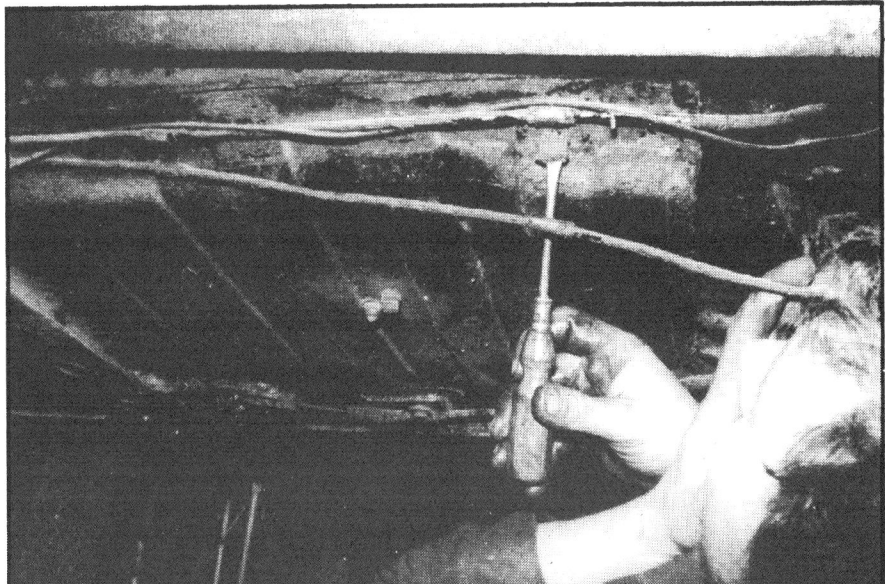

When free, the old line is prised out of the clips or tabs which hold it to the bodyshell.

When installing the new brake lines, try and keep to the manufacturer's original mounting points along the bodyshell — they were probably chosen for a purpose. Several methods of securing the pipes to the body are used, the most common on production cars being little tabs spot-welded to the shell. These sometimes break off however, and you may have to employ new ones of the type supplied by Handy with their kits, which are little brackets with rubber insulation where the pipe runs through them, and which are fixed by self-tappers to the car. In any case, always replace the rubber or plastic insulating pieces otherwise the new brake pipe could vibrate or rub against the body with possibly damaging effects. New insulators can be made from lengths of polythene tube cut up, then slit to enable them to be pushed over the brake line.

If you are restoring the legendary 'basket case' and have no original manufacturer's mounting points to work from, then think out your routine very carefully, avoiding any chance of the brake line being fouled by suspension members, dampers, steering arms and hot exhaust pipes. Test for fouling with the steering on full lock in both directions, and with the suspension on full droop and on as near as full compression as you can get it. Check that your new flexibles can accommodate all this movement too, and aren't touching the wheels or anything else.

A point to bear in mind when doing up brake connectors is not to over-tighten, which will compress the flared ends of the brake pipe too much and could damage an alloy wheel cylinder. The best technique is to do the connector nut up until it stops with little more than the finger-pressure, then do one turn with the spanner. This should be enough to create a good seal. In any case, before the car is taken off its axle stands you should get a helper to maintain a good pressure on the brake pedal while you check every single connection for hydraulic fluid leakage. Now is

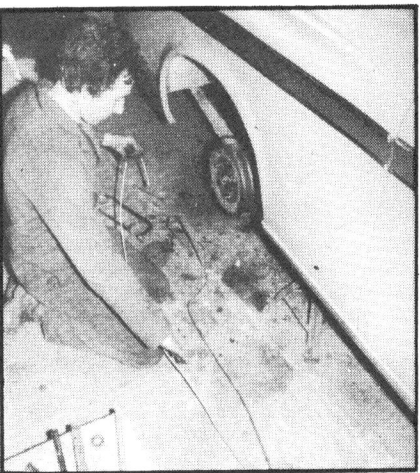

The old pipe is laid on the floor to serve as the pattern for the new length, which is uncoiled and laid alongside.

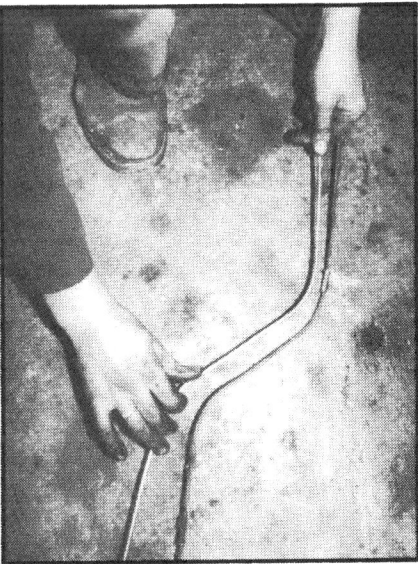

The handy copper piping is easy to bend by hand, following the contours of the original. Note the short lengths of polythene tubing which go over the pipe where it is clipped to the bodyshell — these should be transferred to the new pipe at this stage.

Brake Line Replacement

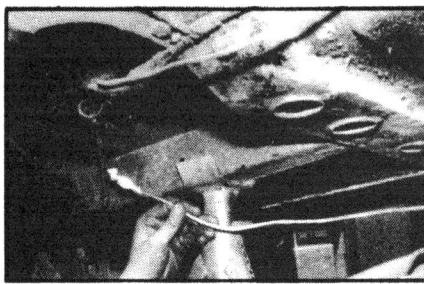

When offering up the correctly bent new piping, cover end with masking tape to both secure connector and to guard against dirt entering.

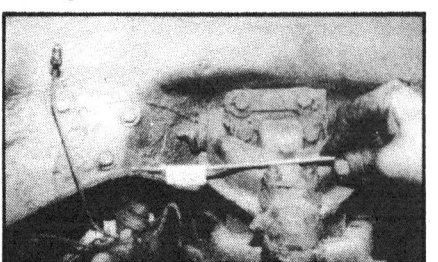

More involved bending operations are usually required near the front suspension — the old pipe from a front wheel cylinder is on the left, and the new one, which has to be shaped to match, is on the right.

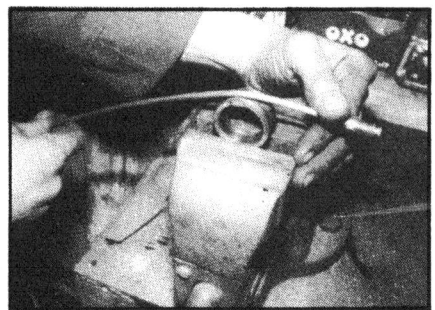

Forming the new tubing around tighter radii is best done on the bench. Here Terry is using the inner part of an old wheel bearing as a former.

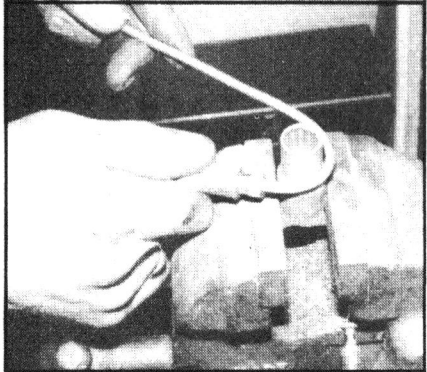

Or you can place a suitable size of socket in the vice and gently curve the brake pipe around that. Don't attempt a bend of less that about 1 ins. radius or you may risk kinking or weakening the pipe.

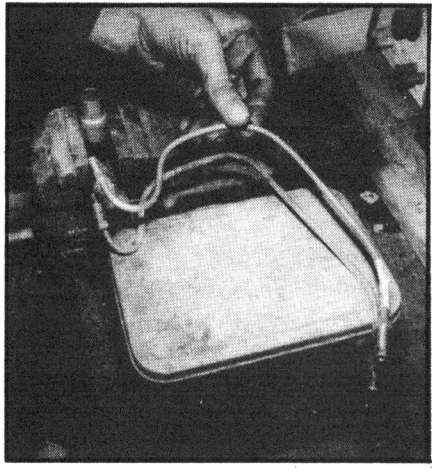

Keep comparing your new length with the old so that you end up with an accurate reproduction.

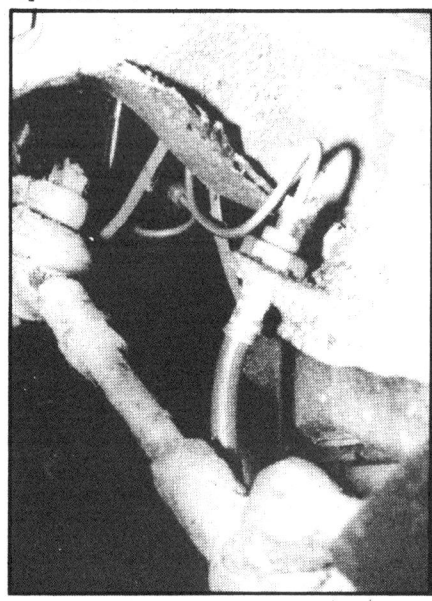

Here is the new pipe in place. By following the original faithfully you should have ensured that nothing will foul it, but check just the same with steering on full lock, and with the suspension under compression, before using the car on the road.

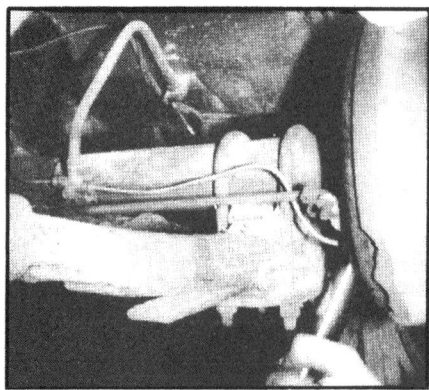

Note that in common with other cars having a 'sliding' rear wheel cylinder, the brake pipe is not clipped to the axle casing after it leaves the inboard union; this allows the movement of the wheel cylinder to be accommodated by a long length of pipe, thus avoiding the chance of fracture by localised 'working' of the metal.

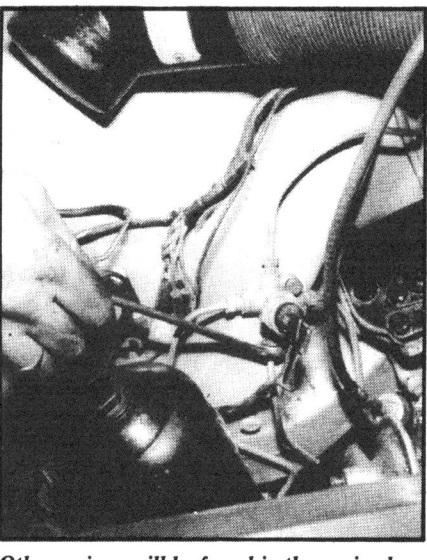

Other unions will be found in the engine bay, where the input from the master cylinder will be distributed to front and rear circuits. Often the brake light switch is situated here, and it is a good idea to check this at the same time as well.

Seized and badly rusted front wheel cylinders caused us to replace the Rapier's caliper units entirely at the front, courtesy of Grimes of Coulsdon. Inserting pads is a bit of a fiddle on this car (they don't slide directly in, but have to be inserted at an angle and then wiggled into position), and it was found easier to do this before fitting the caliper. Discs have been skimmed.

the time to discover this, not out on the road a couple of hundred miles later! This is, of course, assuming that you have thoroughly bled the system, which can be a single-handed operation if you have one of those patent one-way bleeding valves.

We found the copper piping supplied by Handy very easy to use, being flexible and easily bent by hand, using a suitable former where tighter radii were needed. The lengths were all correct and all in all, the job took no more than an afternoon to do.

> **Note:** a complete overhaul of the braking system is an ideal time to change over to silicone brake fluid, which doesn't absorb water to cause rust, and lasts indefinitely. We hope to have news of how you can obtain quantities of this fluid economically in our next issue (see our August 1982 edition for a full report on silicone brake fluid).

Rapier Restoration!

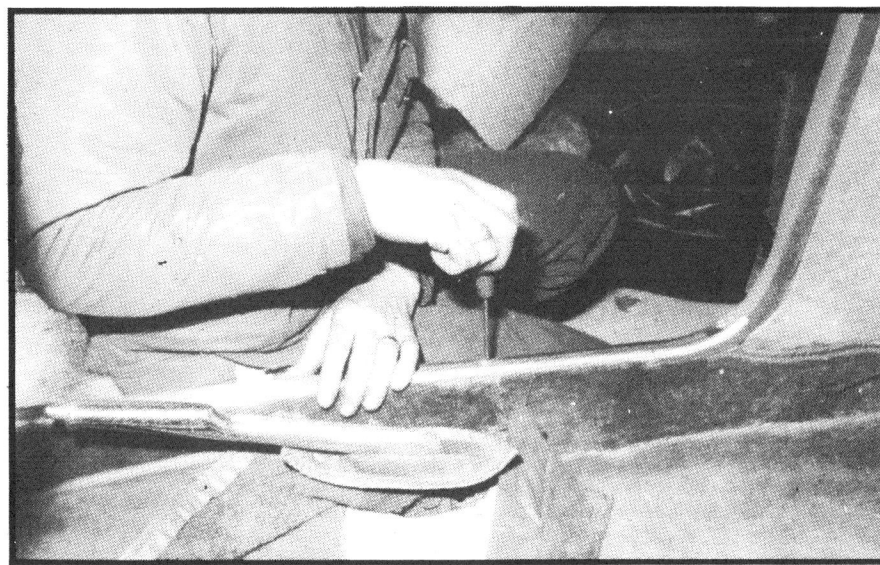

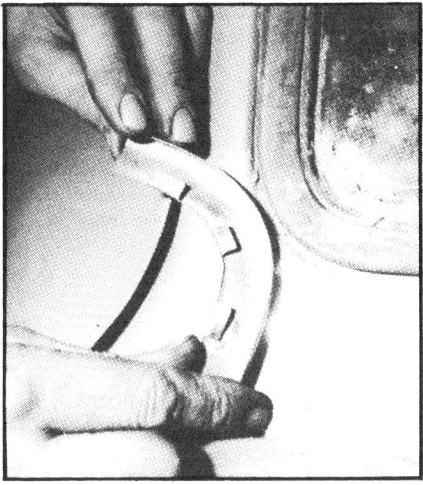

The painters had removed the brightware surround which meant that we had to take out the screen and rubber — the only way to get these very long locating lugs back into the seal, but quite a difficult job.

Putting everything back after a large-scale rebuild is a time-consuming and sometimes an exacting process. Paul Skilleter brings you news on our 1960 Series III.

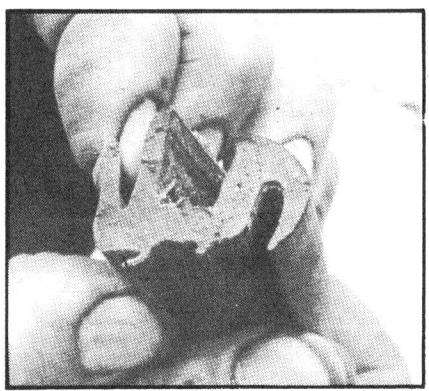

Complex nature of the Rapier's screen rubber is shown here in cross-section; the lip (left) accepts the stainless steel surround. A new rubber was obtained from Grimes of Coulsdon.

O ne of the foremost points which first attracted us to, and caused us to acquire, our Rapier was the condition of its interior. This was, if you remember, in really excellent condition for its age, the seats being untorn, the dashboard wood uncrazed, and even the original carpets being perfectly re-usable given that we weren't intending to produce (in this instance) a totally as-new 'concours' vehicle. So actual re-trim work has been confined to stitching up the odd seperated seam on the seats, cleaning, and — as an experiment — dyeing the carpets.

This last operation was, I suppose, really due to my fetish about original interiors; I admire the craftsmanship of a superbly re-trimmed car (and, as in the case of our Swallow, this is often

the only possibility) but there is nothing quite like an original interior which is exactly as it left the factory. It gives the car great character and I can readily overlook a few blemishes left by age. So I decided to have a go at pepping-up the faded (and admittedly worn in places) carpeting of our Rapier.

The procedure was very easy; I selected a couple of packets of fabric dye at a large store and mixed them up according to the directions, blending a red and an orange to arrive at the particular bright-red hue of our Rapier's carpeting. All the small pieces, and those sections without a heavy backing, were soaked in a large bucket, while the transmission hump and rear carpet (backed by felt) were treated by applying the dye, in more concentrated form, with a cloth, rubbing the dye well into the pile.

The results, after drying in the open air, were very tolerable; the carpets were considerably brighter and cleaner looking,

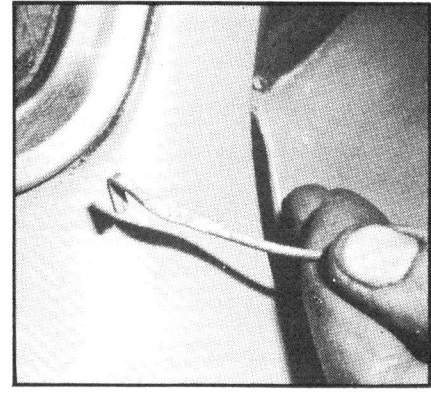

Terry made this little hook for pulling back the rubber lip while inserting the corner pieces of the screen trim, which were the problem ones — the straight pieces could have been inserted with the screen in place.

most of the uneven fading had been disguised, and the very occasional bald patches now had the same colour as the pile, and so could hardly be spotted if you weren't looking for them. Even the Furflex strips were successfully given the treatment! One practical benefit of all this was to save the cost of new carpets, which would not have been inconsiderable as the new set would undoubtedly have had to be made up especially if the original layout was to be duplicated.

Next issue I hope to announce that our Rapier has passed its MoT and undergone something of a road test; I've not driven a Sunbeam Rapier properly before so I'm rather looking forward to that experience. And John Williams, our assistant editor, is even more looking forward to at last getting his 'new' staff car!

Replacing door handles: handle has to be tilted as it goes onto door so that 'bent wire' release mechanism is engaged. Handle is secured by nut up inside the door at either end. Terry points to key number stamped on lock barrel, useful if you've lost the key or are fitting 'new' handles.

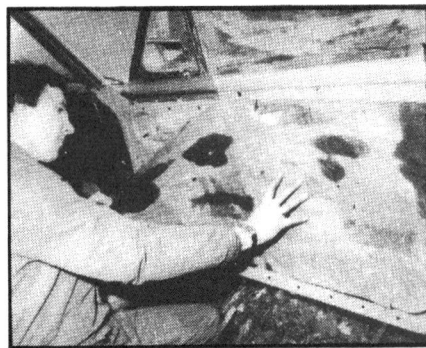

Having rust-proofed the door shell (a procedure on the Rapier to be followed in depth later) the waterproof paper liner is offered up. This prevents the door trim panel getting soggy and so is an important component.

Trim panel follows; about the only point to watch here is the positioning of the clips on the panel, making sure they line up with the holes in the door frame. They are then a simple push-fit.

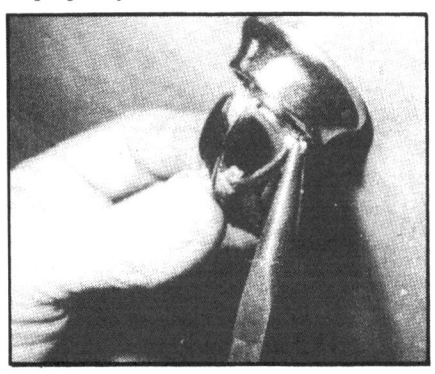

Window winder has sprung inner ring which when pushed down reveals hole in shaft through which pin is inserted. Outer ring has spikes which grip panel. First, put window up and set handle at required angle (usually pointing down). Door handle is secured in same manner.

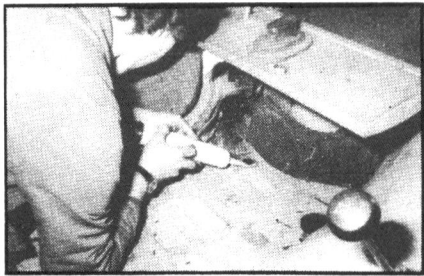

Before fitting carpets, we replaced all grommets and sealed any seams which might admit water.

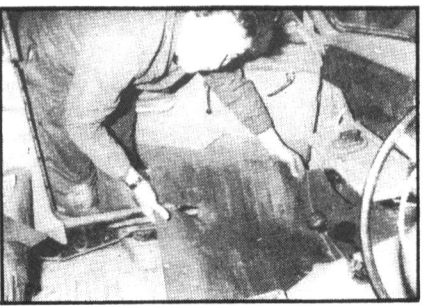

The Rapier is liberally endowed with sound-deadening, the first layer being Mutacell, a thick, tarred paper-like substance.

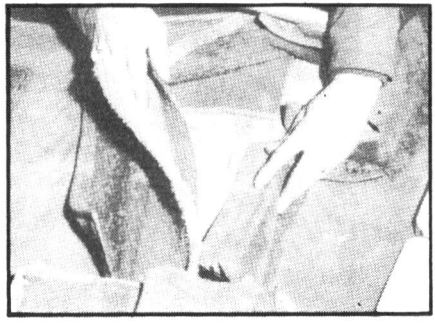

The heavy pieces of under-felt came next, followed by the various carpet shapes.

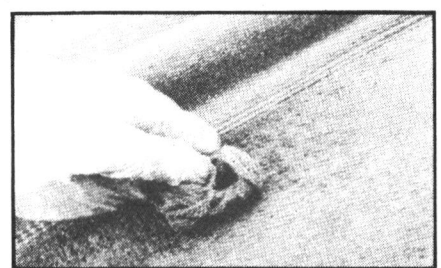

Previously the original carpet had been dyed, the smaller pieces being soaked in a bucket, the larger, felt-backed areas swabbed with a cloth.

The Furflex was in good condition too, and was replaced by simply being pushed onto the seams.

NEXT MONTH
Rust-proofing the Rapier
in preparation for the
winter months

Rust-Proofing Your Restoration

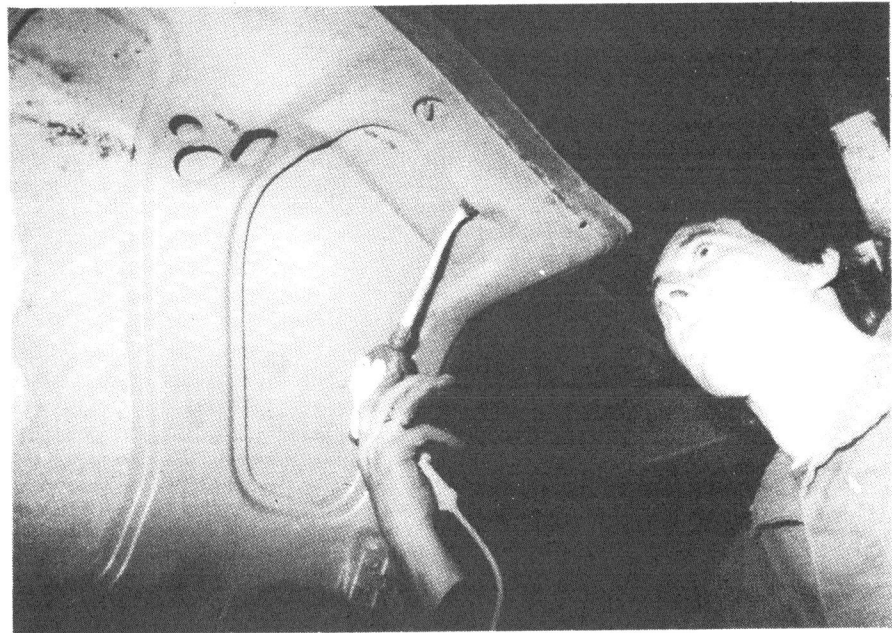

Using our 1960 Sunbeam Rapier as the 'model', Paul Skilleter looks at the techniques you can use to vastly extend the life of your car.

If there is one vital piece of maintenance which I would implore all owners to carry out, having ensured their car is MoT-worthy, it is rust-proofing. Rust is the primary reason why cars end up in the scrap-yard, or become nightmarishly expensive to restore, yet it is simply amazing the number of people who — although not dreaming of missing out any other servicing item — still do not carry out this elementary precaution against the rot which will otherwise destroy their car or their bank-balance (or both). But until the average owner puts rust prevention alongside tasks like oil-changing and polishing, then the sorry story of unnecessary decay and expense will continue.

Low mileage or infrequent use is no guarantee against rot either — I've seen genuine 13,000 and 20,000 mile cars with large holes in them. And while it is obviously best to protect a just-rebuilt or excellent low-

mileage car before rust has really had a chance to set in, even a relatively poor car can benefit enormously from proper treatment, provided it hasn't been affected structurally, as it will help keep it road-worthy and cut down on the eventual body-work repairs.

I've proved the point many times over to my satisfaction on both classic and modern cars — notably my 1962 E-type (now sold) which retains all its original body panels, and my current every-day car, a 1974 Alfa Romeo Alfetta. Most Alfas of this age have rotted to bits, but mine only has rust where my treatment didn't reach. So whatever you own, set aside a few weekends and carry out a systematic rust-proofing operation. You need few tools and not much cash — maybe £20-£30 at the most, or if you're really skint, half that.

The principles behind successful rust-proofing are simple. Firstly, you must know your car's bodywork construction inside out, so that you can protect every enclosed area, and every mud-collecting seam, lip or cavity. It is a great help if you look at really poor examples of 'your' make too, and note the trouble spots down for extra attention; try visiting the scrap-yard if you have a 60s/70s vehicle, for this reason.

Secondly, when it comes to the underside,

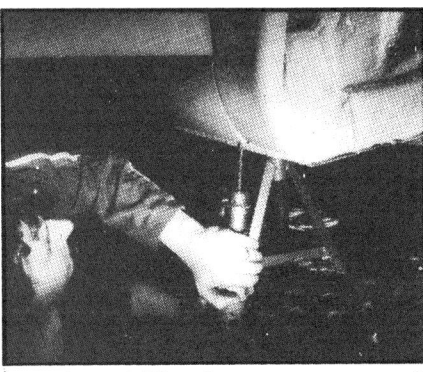

Sometimes drilling is necessary to reach enclosed sections having no other access holes; here the outer sill of the Rapier is being penetrated. The hole will also serve as a drain, so will be left unplugged.

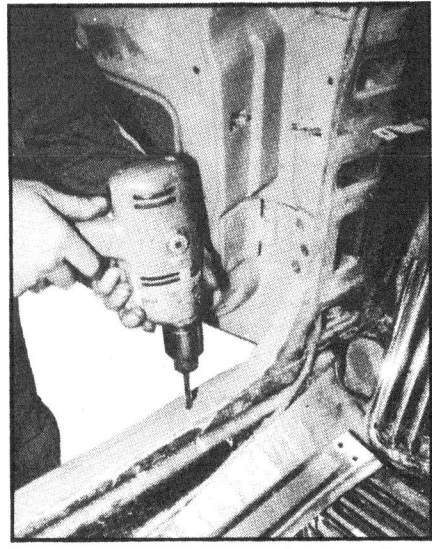

The Rapier's sill construction includes a middle diaphragm or 'wall', so the cavity both sides of this have to be treated separately. Here Terry drills the top face of the door step prior to injecting the inner cavity.

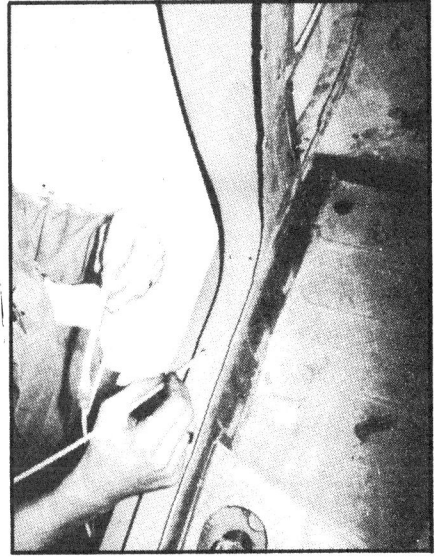

A similar hole is drilled in the inner section of the door step at the rear, to ensure complete coverage. Flexible probe is used to get the material distributed properly inside.

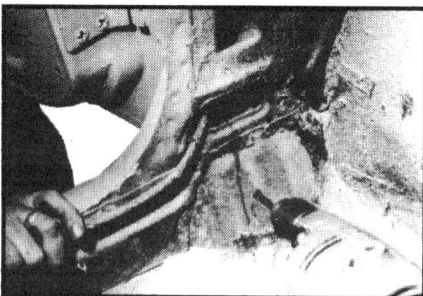

The Rapier has a strengthening fillet adjacent to the hinge pillar which needs to be drilled separately; the original one had rotted out so protection was essential.

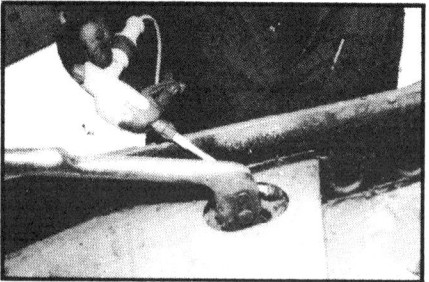

Everywhere that water may lay must be treated; this area is covered by rubber gaiter (NB: anyone have a new or usable gaiter? — ours has perished) but water could still get in from below.

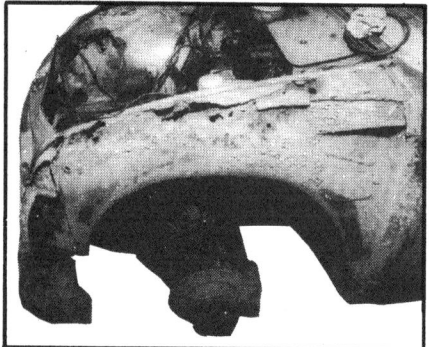

The classic mud-trap on the Rapier/Minx range is the shelf formed by the inner wing wall curving inwards at the top. Mud collects and causes this sort of havoc as owners know only too well.

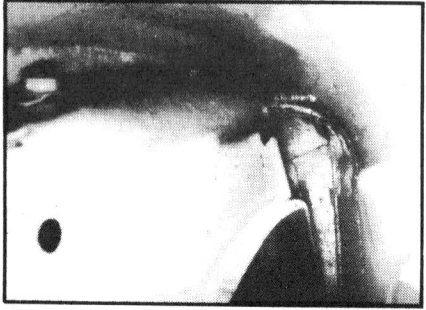

This is the same area on our repaired car, looking from the front and with the outer wing in place. The 'shelf' was heavily coated with both under-sealant and Waxoyl, but as the car is to be an every-day workhorse for a while, we intend closing off this area with an aluminium or plastic panel.

you can't protect properly, if there's dirt around. Invest in having the car steam cleaned (£5 - £8), or resign yourself to getting dirty and spend a day with hose-pipe, loo brush and old paintbrush to get the muck out of corners and crevices (don't be too fussy about large flat areas if the sealant is sound — they never rot through because there's nowhere for moisture to be held against the metal). Even after a steam clean you will still need to get mud out of the trickier corners underneath, however. In fact, this cleaning operation itself will extend the life of the vehicle, particularly if you keep it clean thereafter with a fortnightly hosing down underneath.

The third stage is applying the under-body protection, having taken the car for a run to dry it off. Again, concentrate on corners and crevices first. If the car is to be actively used during the winter, I find that good old Underseal is best for areas subjected to road dirt abrasion — even Waxoyl gets blasted off the panelwork immediately behind the wheels, I find. But the surface to which it's applied must be rust-free, so scrape rust off first (an angle-grinder is ideal for this). I also use a mixture of sealant and Waxoyl under the car too, the former giving more 'body', the latter hopefully providing a rust-killing capacity. Having treated the danger spots, spray the entire underside with a nice loose solution of Waxoyl, Black Knight or Tectyl.

Stage four is protecting the box-members. This can be done without any preliminary cleaning and if you are too lazy to go about cleaning the underside, at least carry this operation out as it will add years to the structural life of your car even if it won't prevent the wings falling off. Unitary contruction cars are built in very similar ways and the main places to treat are examplified by our Rapier. Again, careful examination will reveal where you should inject; very often you will be able to locate existing holes (maybe covered with grommets) to use for this purpose, otherwise don't be afraid of drilling — preferably where the hole will be covered by a step-plate although don't worry too much, as a neat little plug in a door pillar is far preferable to a gaping hole in a few years' time.

There is one fairly major problem with internal protection when the subject vehicle is old, and that's the tendency for dirt, rust scale, and bits of old sealant to collect at the bottom of the sill or box section to be treated (especially where these lie just behind a road wheel). If you are lucky enough to have a car with a removable closing plate or large rubber bung in these areas, remove it and clear all the debris you can, using any device you can dream up that will reach inside and pull out the rubbish. Otherwise (and I've cut open sills to establish this exact point) the rust-proofing material tends to lay on top of the debris, or is absorbed by it, and thus is prevented from getting to the metal underneath and protecting it.

A danger-point shared by most cars is behind the front wheel — mud thrown up by the wheel collects in the corners formed between wings, hinge pillar and bulkhead, holds the damp, and quickly rots them out. A heavy material to withstand abrasion should be the protective medium used here and in the rear wheel arch.

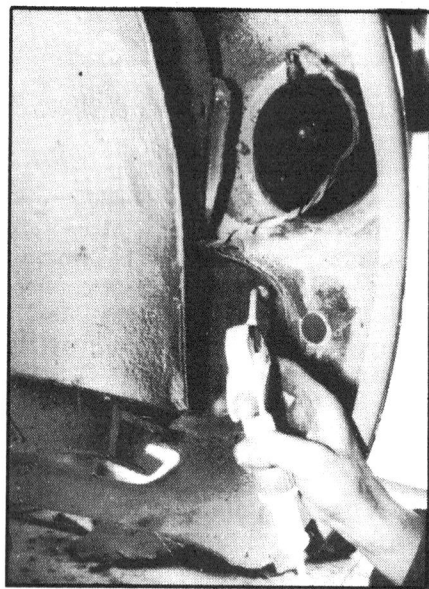

Many wings have seams and ledges at the front, around and below the headlight bowl. All should be extensively protected against water and mud. Those wing lips must also be given a thick coating where they curl over to form additional mud-traps.

Stage five is routine maintenance — add rust-proofing to your major service schedule, so that your car's underside is regularly cleaned (much easier that way), and is re-injected at least every two years. While polishing the car (which itself does nothing to preserve it, remember), dribble Tectyl or similar down outer body seams and squirt it

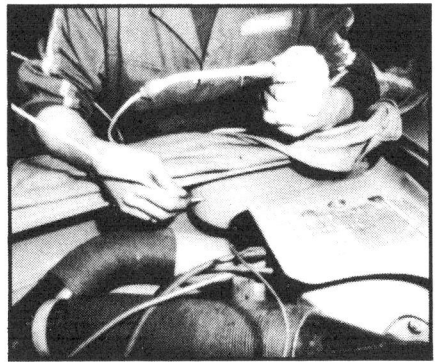

To get into the box section which triangulates the inner wing and bulkhead (see previous 'before' picture), we drilled this curved member under the bonnet and used the probe.

Like most unitary construction cars, the Rapier/Minx has built-in chassis box-members; these must be injected along their length, although here, alongside the engine, oil normally prevents rot occuring. Watch the front cross-member under the radiator though — this often suffers.

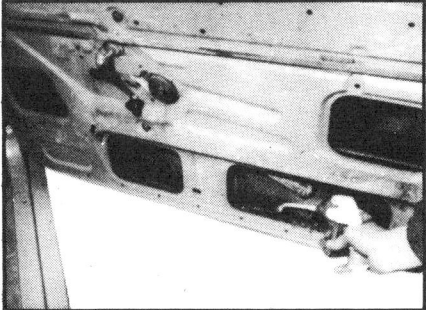

Having protected all door pillars, the doors themselves must not be neglected. Much the best way is to completely remove the door trim and liners, so that loose debris can be removed and the rust-proofing material applied exactly where it is needed most.

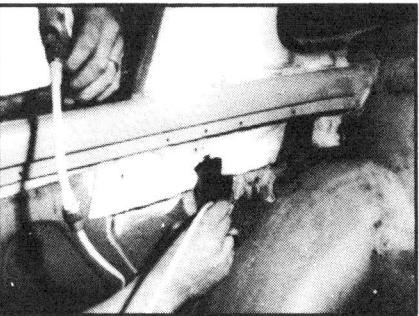

A highly vunerable area on virtually all cars is the 'V' formed where inner and outer wings meet around the wheel-arch. This can easily be treated from inside the car after the removal of trim panels; here the extension is pushed right into the 'V' and copious amounts of fluid injected.

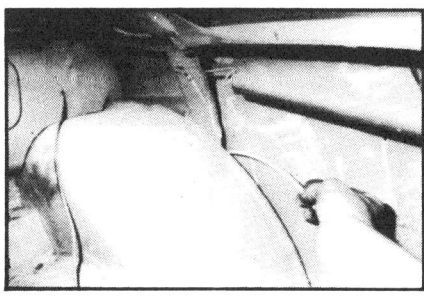

On most cars too, the rear wheel arch extends into the boot where the protection can be continued. Removal of the side trim panels will also allow treatment of the rear wing/boot floor cavity aft of the wheel-arch. Bootlid and bonnet should be treated as well, don't forget, and around and under the petrol tank and spare wheel well if exposed.

behind bumpers. Take out the side-light units and treat them too — even if they are plastic, because the bulb-holders and earthing strips inside are not. If you have a real 'working' vehicle that is going to be out on the salt-laden roads all the winter with little likelihood of being cleaned, protect the chrome with WD 40 or even slightly thinned Waxoyl; if this is kept up it will preserve the bightware like new until the summer, when it can be cleaned off with white spirit.

WHAT TO USE

The best-known rust-proofer is Waxoyl, obtainable by mail order direct from the manufacturers (Finnigans) or in recent years from retail outlets too. It is applied with a hand-trigger squirter using either a nozzle or a probe. Like most other products of its type, I find it best to heat the material well, by placing the can in a bucket of very hot water for 15 minutes — it becomes much easier to apply and more penetrating. I also like to dilute it up to 30% with white spirit for the first application inside box members, to increase its flow and creeping properties. Recently Finnigans gave their product more body which lessened its tendency to run — I

rather preferred the original more liquid type, as you could hear it dripping and running inside the sill or whatever, really getting to the places where water would get to. 'Black' Waxoyl is also now available, giving a presentable finish to the underside of the car.

Black Knight are rivals to Waxoyl, and appear to be doing quite well. I have less experience with this product but it appears to be effective. Two different grades are available, the heavier one being for under body protection.

Tectyl is made by Valvoline and is extensively used in the steel industry to protect new steel. You can buy it in very useful aerosol form, or in greater (gallon or more) quantities from Sound Services of 55 West End, Witney, Oxon (Tel: 0993 4981), whose proprietors happen to have a passion for Mk X Jaguars! Two grades are available, one for underbody protection again, but I find the 'ML' lighter material ideal for not only injecting sound metal cavities, but also for running down body seams and behind chrome. It sets harder than Waxoyl or Black Knight, but can still be removed by white spirit.

Finally, you have 'Fertan & Overs', made by an Italian based company and unique in that a multiple process is used. A rust neutraliser (which appears similar in constituency to Trustan) is thus first applied, followed after curing by a wax-type substance. This product appears to be good, although I cannot report yet on its long-term performance. The biggest problem with using a nuetraliser is that in enclosed sections like sills, it would tend to get absorbed by the rubbish which as already mentioned is usually inside.

In a different catagory are the conventional under-body sealants, of which the trade-mark 'Underseal' is just one. They are very cheap, and effective if applied to clean, non-rusted steel. These products got a bad name in the late fifties/sixties because in old age they tended to harden and then separated from the metal, allowing in water which quickly produced rot. If the existing sealant on your

The Morris Minor and the Sunbeam Tiger in the picture are in the process of receiving the Waxoyl treatment at the workshops of Ferroguard, who use only Finnigans products. Ferroguard can be found at Old Hathern Railway Station, Normanton Upon Soar, Loughborough, Leics., and their telephone number is Loughborough 842560.

car has not separated, all you need do is spray it with Waxoyl or Black Knight Rust-Stop which will soften it and prolong its life still further. Under-body sealants are best used where, as already explained, the body is subjected to buffeting from road dirt.

Well, if you carry out some or all of the above, you will be rewarded with a car which will defy old-age so far as much of its bodywork is concerned. And remember that if you don't, there's going to be only one result — rot . . . . ☐

Rallyi
Rebuil

It must have been at least ten years ago that I remember discussing with a *Motoring News* man, during coverage of some national rally, the attractive idea of getting historic cars into rallying; this was at a time when the racing of '50s and '60s machinery had got well into its stride and, we reasoned, wouldn't it be nice if rally cars from this and the pre-war period could be seen performing too? A suggestion then was that a class for historic cars could be included in one of the existing major rallies — like the RAC or the Welsh — with the old cars running on just the non-damaging tarmac sections; this way advantage could have been taken of an existing organisational structure, an event within an event as it were.

Nothing came of this however, for the very good reason that no-one, including me, did anything more about it. In any case, latching onto a big rally would probably have caused more problems than it would have solved. But then came the RAC 'Golden Fifty' of 1982, a three-day event for historic roadgoing cars to celebrate fifty years of the RAC Rally. And that really did start something....

The 'Golden Fifty' was followed by the Silver Jubilee rally the same year organised by the Association of Welsh Motor Clubs, and it brought a similarly enthusiastic response from owners of pre-1967 cars. All this had not passed unnoticed at *Practical Classics*, so when Jeremy Dickson, secretary of the Welsh Counties Car Club, wrote to us in March of this year saying they intended to revive the Coronation Rally (first held in 1953) and turn it into an 'historic' event, the temptation to enter something in it was very strong.

The 'something' really had to be the 1960 Sunbeam Rapier we'd originally bought from a scrapman for £50 and then rebuilt as a 'Project Car' during 1982; a very original car to start with, the engine had been rebuilt, the overdrive replaced and the brakes largely renewed, so that mechanically it was in fine shape. We decided at the outset we would make no attempt to modify the car, but just make absolutely certain that everything was working as the manufacturer intended — and I reckon this alone generally puts you ahead of a good many other competitors! The sole deviation from standard was the fitment of Spax adjustable shock absorbers all round, and which indeed were to prove worth their weight in gold.

So much for preparation of the car (of which John tells more later on); the crew were much less ready and frankly as August 13th drew near and the final regulations arrived, I didn't rate our chances of finishing very highly. Not really because of any drastic driving error, but more because of us making some silly navigational mistake and getting excluded on lateness at a control. Neither John — who I'd cruelly nominated as

In the first of an occasional series about classic car and John Williams tell how we entered our 1960 form of historic motor sport — and survived!

ACTION

...ng a ...d!

...n action, Paul Skilleter ...nbeam Rapier in a new

navigator — nor I had any experience of rallies, you see, so initially the whole thing was a bit of a mystery to us. In years past I'd covered many a rally as a staff photographer for *Motor*, but spectating is vastly different from taking part....

Not that I was a total beginner to motor sport itself; I at least had the advantage of a number of seasons' racing and hill-climbing my XK120 roadster a few years back, plus some classic saloon car racing in a 2.4 Jaguar. So I was used to driving against the clock and in older-type cars. I was even fairly used to Welsh roads, thanks to many 'Motor' magazine group tests during my years with that journal — although there is no way you can really compare even the fastest public-road driving to competition driving. I'm not sure that the long-suffering John Williams quite appreciated this fact before the event; he did after the first special stage, however!

The evening before the event was pleasantly spent chatting to our fellow competitors; the variety of cars was delightful and ranged from David Hescroft's splendid AC 16/80 of around 1935, through MGAs, A35s, an A40 and a 105E Anglia to the big Healeys, very rapid Lotus Cortinas, and ex-works Mini Coopers — the favourites for overall best performance. Amongst the latter was

Flying finish! Our Rapier nears the end of a special stage; we expected the car to bottom on sections like this, but it never did. Photo: Geoff Le Provost.

Gethin Jones with his very original ex-works Cooper 'S', co-driven by Martin Pearce of the Midlands Mini Centre who helped us so much with the rebuild of our 998 Cooper Project Car (see elsewhere in this issue). The Rapier passed its scrutineering with no problems and we went to bed determined that in the morning, whatever else may transpire, we would have some fun.

The start ceremony was just that — an informal send-off at the Castle Hotel, Llandovery largely for the benefit of spectators. The real event began on the Epynt army ranges some 32 miles away, with a gentle introduction in the form of a driving test round cones. I put John in the driving seat for this, as I suffer from mental blanks during this sort of thing and forget which way I'm supposed to go, and 'wrong slotting' meant a maximum time penalty. John reeled off the test with great efficiency and we moved onto Test 3, a 'regularity run'; here we had to proceed for exactly one mile at 25 mph, and thereafter at exactly 30 mph to the unspecified finish.

It was here that I did my only bit of navigating. Gethin Jones (tragically his Mini suffered a broken diff after the first test) had kindly given us a chart which indicated in seconds what each tenth of a mile should take for both the required speeds. So all I had to do was set my trip to '0', and start the stop-watch to read off the seconds at each tenth and tell John to go faster or slower. I

failed to do either. We made the mistake of driving straight up to the start of this test without doing up seat belts and organising ourselves generally, and suddenly we were told "20 seconds to go" before we were ready; the results was as mentioned and we ended up travelling the distance at much too high a speed and incurring an 11 second penalty. First lesson: unless you're running late, don't go to the start until you are absolutely ready to go....

Test 3 was an 0.8 mile hillclimb, the first speed section in the rally. We tightened our helmets and waited for the marshall to begin the count-down — 5, 4, 3, 2, 1, GO! It was simply a matter of traversing the climbing road ahead of us to the flying finish as quickly as possible. Revs at around 4,500 and drop the clutch — and my heart sank because the engine note hardly dropped in response. We had clutch slip, and badly, and it continued as I pushed the lever into second. Oh no, I thought, we're out of the rally before we've even really started; because in my experience, once a clutch begins to slip you can bet that under competitive conditions it isn't going to last more than a few minutes.

But as we made our rather sedate progress up the hill — the Rapier isn't exactly quick, and the slipping clutch had ruined a good attacking start — I couldn't detect any tell-tale smell of burning clutch linings, which gave us a glimmer of hope. It might just be oil mist, and if so, it should burn off and the plates grip again. Sure enough, on the next test, which was another hill climb, the grip was better and it continued to improve thereafter. Our luck was in, at least initially.

Then came our first special stage — the experience of driving flat out on narrow, undulating Welsh roads without having to worry about traffic coming the other way. Here the true qualities of the Rapier began to become evident; its 1500cc engine couldn't convey much in the way of acceleration, but I quickly became aware that the car's handling was amazingly good for its age and type. After all, a Rapier is only a mildly warmed Hillman 'Series' Minx but I am still filled with admiration at its controllability on those skinny tyres.

Taken straight from everyday motoring as John William's staff car, the Rapier needed little attention before the start. Here John fixes the rally plate and I attempt to make sense of the road book.

Rallying a Rebuild!

Of course the predominant handling characteristic was, typically, strong understeer, perhaps even more evident in the Rapier/Minx family than in other contemporary family saloons, and in its period this was the main handicap to be overcome when the Rapier was raced and rallied. We had done what we could to minimise this by setting the Spax dampers harder at the front than the rear, and by running higher pressures in the front tyres, and this did help to stiffen the front and cut down front tyre scrub on corners. But very rarely did the tail slide on the tarmac surfaced roads we were driving on, which you really need to have happen on a rally car so that you can change direction more quickly.

On the other hand though, you can take greater liberties in throwing around an understeering car, especially if you are not experienced in a rally situation, and for me at any rate the Rapier was nearly ideal as there was little danger of 'losing' the rear end irrevocably and ending up in the undergrowth. On the contrary — enter a corner a little too fast and speed was soon scrubbed off by the front tyres; a sort of safety valve.

In all there were 15 tests, of which about a dozen were special stages or hill climbs; we didn't do too well on the latter, or where straight line speed counted, as its power/weight ratio is not one of the Rapier's outstanding points. However, thanks to the predictable and consistent handling I think we acquitted ourselves reasonably on the remainder, until....

Mechanically, the car seemed fine up to past the half-way stage of the event; the engine was on song and the overdrive proved most useful, allowing rapid changes from third to overdrive third and back. In fact overdrive third, slightly lower than direct top, was the highest ratio I used — I daresay I could have snatched top on occasions but there always seemed to be a blind brow looming, and I am not very brave when it comes to that sort of "hope there's not a right-angle bend over this" type motoring. But the previously faithful engine gradually began to loose power, and despite ministrations by Geoff, soon went onto three if not 2½ cylinders.

Naturally, this drastically affected our times for the last few stages. In particular, the final one, a marvellous 5.40 mile 'blind' through superb countryside, was completed with a very sick engine, though on reflection it was probably our best effort as despite losing at least one cylinder, *and* coming up

Jeremy Dickson of the Welsh Counties Car Club lifts the flag, and we're off. John takes the wheel for the drive to Mynd Epynt.

behind a neatly driven but slow A35, *and* our only excursion onto the grass when I tried to take an uphill bend a little too quickly in trying to make up time, we noted afterwards that we'd only dropped 23 seconds on our closest rival, the hard-driven Jowett Jupiter of Mike Smailes and Geoff McAuley, on that section. I guess the A35 was worth that much alone.

Tired but happy, to coin a phrase, we returned to base at the Castle Hotel and went off to get fish and chips, not thinking we'd figured in the results; only to learn after we arrived back as the prize giving ended that we'd actually achieved 3rd in class behind the modified MGA of Adam Wiseberg and John Halton, and the Jupiter. Our position overall was 25th out of approximately 60 starters — not bad for a genuinely standard 1½ litre saloon, and it certainly brought home to John and I exactly why the Rapier was such a suc-

The camera never lies! John did all the autotest driving, although like most people incurred a few penalties by clipping a cone.

cessful rally car in its day. Stamina (our carb. problems aside) and safe handling count for a lot, obviously.

Not everyone was so happy; a feature of this event was an encouragingly large entry from classic saloon and 'thoroughbred' or MG championship racing people, mostly with modified cars. These were extremely quick and some of the experienced rally drivers competing were visibly shaken by some of their initial stage times. But a number of the newcomers tried just a little too hard on unknown roads and round blind bends, and consequently not a few went off, some — like John Chatham who rolled his works-replica Healey 3000 — lucky to escape serious injury. We ourselves came across some horrific skid marks on a particularly trickey lefthander, and rounded the corner to see the Morgan of Kevin Donnelly and Mike Ridley hundreds of yards down the hillside... But miraculously the car had remained upright and they even finished the course. Mike had recently sold the Morgan to Kevin and was driving it at the time — but they were still talking to each other later in the day!

Even with such escapades, the Coronation Rally was adjudged to be a resounding success, and I for one am deeply thankful to Jeremy Dickson and all his marshalls and helpers in the Welsh Counties Car Club who went out of their way to make us newcomers feel at home and enjoy ourselves. They were all tremendously enthusiastic about their magnificent special stage roads and I feel very privileged to have had the opportunity of experiencing for myself the unique sort of competitive motoring they allow. Compara-

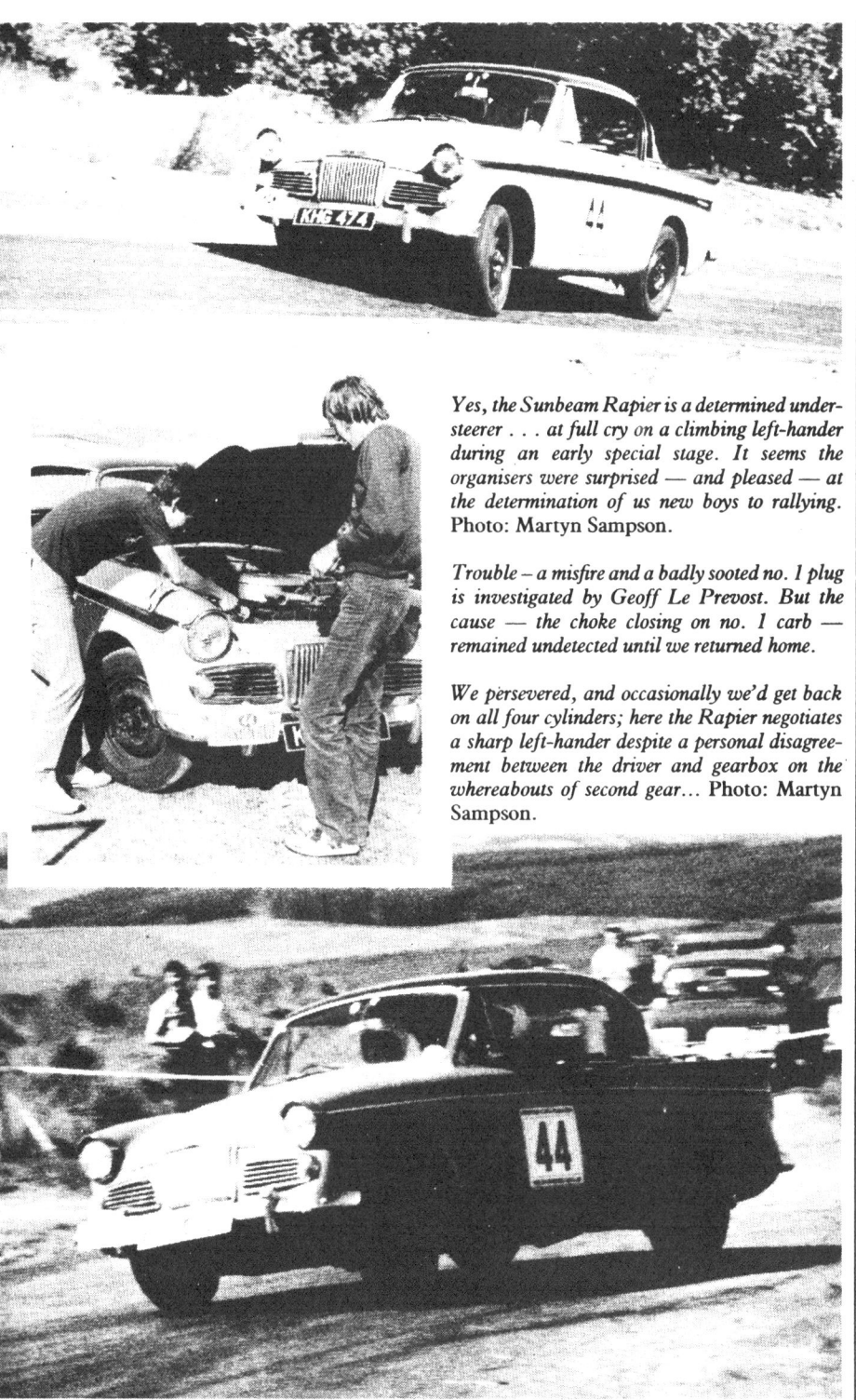

Yes, the Sunbeam Rapier is a determined understeerer . . . at full cry on a climbing left-hander during an early special stage. It seems the organisers were surprised — and pleased — at the determination of us new boys to rallying. Photo: Martyn Sampson.

Trouble – a misfire and a badly sooted no. 1 plug is investigated by Geoff Le Prevost. But the cause — the choke closing on no. 1 carb — remained undetected until we returned home.

We persevered, and occasionally we'd get back on all four cylinders; here the Rapier negotiates a sharp left-hander despite a personal disagreement between the driver and gearbox on the whereabouts of second gear... Photo: Martyn Sampson.

tively few rallies include genuine special stages over closed roads, and it must be quite rare for a total beginner to try his hand at such on his very first event.

John and I certainly hope that the rally will be repeated, and even improved given the experience of this pilot event. Congratulations too to Phillip Young and *Sporting Cars* for giving their backing and thus helping it become a reality. Yes, historic rallying is enormous fun, you can enter virtually any type of pre-1967 car (with very little modification if you so desire), and the entry fee of

£35 was modest compared with the entertainment you get from it all. I think we'll take part again if we get the opportunity — if only to prove that our Project Car rebuilds really don't fall apart if asked to repeat the activities their contemporaries undertook in international rallies all those years ago! *POS*

The navigator's tale.

When I agreed to the suggestion that my staff car, the 1960 Series III Sunbeam Rapier, should be entered in the Coronation Rally on

August 13th, I had no idea what I was letting myself in for, nor indeed very much idea of what rallying was about. In *Practical Classics* we have paid a great deal of attention to buying and restoring classic, and some not-so-classic, cars and I had already expressed the view that we should take a closer look at how the cars can be, and are, used; so I could hardly decline an invitation to be at the sharp end of our first excursion into competitive motoring.

It was understood from the outset that Paul Skilleter was to be the driver. Having never been driven by Paul until the day before the rally it was reassuring to me to know that he had done a fair amount of racing in Jaguars (admittedly a few years ago) and would therefore (I thought) ensure that we achieved a reasonable result in our first attempt at rallying without putting my staff car (not to mention me) at risk by indulging in the sort of undignified antics which are usually described as 'rearranging the scenery'.

Preparation

Newcomers to rallying soon discover that the preparation for an event entails rather more than simply ensuring that the car is roadworthy and the sandwiches are packed. The Royal Automobile Club through the RAC Motor Sports Association Ltd is the governing body for motor sport in the United Kingdom and the MSA regulations are, to say the least, extensive. They can be found in the current issue of the RAC British Motor Sports Yearbook and although the task may at first appear daunting it is well worth studying all the relevant sections of this book, making notes of those items which will require attention. Each entrant in a particular event also receives supplementary regulations from the organisers of the event some time before the event, and a few days before the event final instructions are issued.

The car had been serviced and the brakes overhauled some weeks before the Coronation Rally, but we wanted to carry out further improvments before the event. In particular the carburettors needed attention — they were (and are) very worn but we had been unable to track down any new replacements. So we took the car to Southern Carburettors at Wimbledon where a few defects were discovered and rectified and a very fine job was made of tuning, resulting in a great improvment in performance.

Previously the acceleration had been little better than satisfactory up to 3000 rpm, but very impressive at higher engine speeds. After the visit to Southern Carburettors, the acceleration at higher speeds was just as impressive, but there was a great deal more 'pull' at low engine speeds.

It had never been our intention to carry out major alterations or additions to the car, but merely to rally it in normal road going form with the addition of such safety equipment as we thought reasonable or the regulations demanded. We fitted lap and diagonal seat belts, but the supplementary regulations indicated that roll-over bars would be recom-

This shot illustrates very well the meandering roads over the Epynt army ranges; brilliant weather added to our enjoyment too. Photo: Martyn Sampson.

Rallying a Rebuild!

mended rather than mandatory on this particular event. We allowed ourselves a full set of adjustable shock absorbers and chose Spax because they could be adjusted so easily on the car without any dismantling. These made a tremendous difference to the steering and road holding; the original shock absorbers (although in very good condition) couldn't possibly have coped with the speeds at which

we were able to cover the hillclimbs and special stages with the Spax. Individual throttle return springs (required by the regulations and supplied by Southern Carburettors) were fitted to each carburettor — these are intended to close the throttles automatically in the event of accelerator linkage failure and I was pleased to discover that they had virtually no effect on the pressure needed on the

RESULTS SUMMARY
Overall winner calculated using Performance Index:
Car No. 7 Don Pither/Chris Baron, Sunbeam Tiger

The Top 15 based on time

Car No.	Crew	Total Time	Car
20	David Thomas/Jeff Hignett	32.22	Mini Clubman
43	Dave Wheeler/John Evans	32.29	Renault 8 Gordini
31	Steve Griggs/Dave Jenkins	32.44	Mini Cooper 'S'
51	Peter Harries/Russell Thomas	32.59	Mini Cooper 'S'
42	Tony Morgan/Roger Evans	33.04	Mini Cooper 'S'
9	Adam Wiseberg/John Halton	33.20	MGA
39	Ryan Morris/Clive Morris	33.20	Mini Cooper
56	Andy Elcomb/Graham Child	33.24	Triumph 2000
21	Peter Russell/Steve Foster	33.38	Porsche 911
10	Alan McKay Firth/David Hunter	33.48	Lotus Cortina
27	Denis Gardell/Stuart Cardell	34.15	Mini Cooper 'S'
38	Steve Marks/Barbara Marks	34.23	Lotus Elan
26	Doug Griffiths/Phil Barry	34.27	Morris Minor
49	Brian Davies/Elwyn Sugden	34.33	Lotus Cortina
29	Robert Cameron/Robert Fletcher	35.18	Rover 2000

Our car (25th overall):

Car No.	Crew	Total Time	Car
44	Paul Skilleter/John Williams	37.44	Sunbeam Rapier S3

Class Winners

Car No.	Crew	Class	Car
3	David Hescroff/Nigel Phillips	A2	AC 16/80
9	Adam Wiseberg/John Halton	B5	MGA
41	Michael Knowles/Michael Tucker	B6	Austin Healey 3000
31	Steve Griggs/Dave Jenkins	C7	Mini Cooper 'S'
21	Peter Russell/Steve Foster	C8	Porsche 911
7	Don Pither/Chris Baron	C9	Sunbeam Tiger
20	David Thomas/Jeff Hignett	D12	Mini Clubman

The high-flying MGA of Adam Wiseberg and John Halton, normally seen in MGCC circuit racing, which won our class, 4 mins 24 secs ahead of us.

We weren't clued-up enough at the time to notice it, but our closest rival in Class B5 (1941-1960 up to 2000cc) was the Jupiter of Mike Smailes and Geoff McAuley, another car to show its pedigree — we were 2 minutes behind at the end. The smart Magnette is the Pearce/Carter car.

accelerator pedal.

The Rapier's front seat needed attention to comply with the regulation which states that seats should not fold. Then, a few days before we set off for Wales I delivered the car to Dermody Garage in Lewisham with instructions to ensure that everything was tightly screwed in place and to make and fit a sump guard.

The MSA regulations indicated that a red reflective warning triangle would be needed, plus not less than 5 kg of fire extinguishant (BCF or BTM) in not more than two units, and I would need a helmet to British Standard BS2495:1977. A triangle was found in the seventh accessory shop I tried, fire extinguishers are not necessarily available, or available in suitable sizes even from specialist racing and competition equipment suppliers (and we were quoted between £24 and £40 for the 2½ kg size). Just to be awkward I wanted an open face helmet — this type seems to be going out of fashion — but eventually found one at Road and Racing Accessories Ltd (01-736 2881), where it is worth noting that the service was unusually polite and efficient — in contrast to the all-too-prevalent couldn't care less attitudes encountered elsewhere.

The final preparations to the car were carried out at the Castle Hotel, Llandovery, in the hours before the rally started. The final adjustments were made to the shock absorbers, the rally plates and numbers and backgrounds were attached to the car (these had been supplied by the organisers) having first applied extra polish to the relevant panels so that the adhesive would not get too firm a grip on the paintwork. The front number plate (the lowest part of the car) was raised and mounted on the front bumper.

The road book

Before our visit to Wales I had read the recently-published book 'Rally Navigation' by Martin Holmes in the hope of obtaining a clearer idea of what happens on a rally. No doubt this informative book would have been more helpful to me had I read it with some prior knowledge of what form the Coronation Rally would take. All was revealed the night before the rally when we had the car scrutineered, and signed on and were given the road book. This contained all the information which we would need on the three autotests (diagrams included), two regularity sections, three hillclimbs and seven special stages of which the rally was comprised. The routes which we were to follow were indicated by means of "Tulip" symbols against a running total of the mileage covered, and although we had obtained the recommended ordnance survey maps we really didn't need them.

What was it like?

Prior to the event I had learnt that in 'serious' rallying the navigator/co-driver needed to possess certain qualities, including a completely unreasonable degree of fearlessness and a cast iron stomach, and I would lay claim to neither of these. In theory my job was simple, all I had to do during the 'fast bits', that is the hillclimbs and special stages, was to keep a sharp eye on the trip mileage counter and shout directions to the driver (based on the directions in the road book) in advance of the major changes of direction at road junctions. Simple? Well, yes, if you allow for the fact that at speed on narrow, twisting, undulating mountain roads the car becomes a demented cocktail shaker and the navigator in particular (not being intimately involved in the actual driving) is the ingredients. I became accustomed to this quite quickly, in fact as quickly as I convinced myself, for want of a better reason, that there was a job to do and that our survival, let alone success, could depend upon it.

During the first couple of speed events I was most disinclined to enjoy the view out of the windows, this merely served to remind me of a growing conviction that "The End was near", but I am bound to say that this feeling was in turn overcome by a growing admiration for both car and driver. I really had no idea that our Rapier could be made to move so fast and especially around corners and bends, irrespective of an assorted combination of gradients, not do I understand even now how a car which seems to have little or no contact with the road can be persuaded to accomplish a complete change of direction in fractions of a second. I soon began to find the events immensely exciting, and, yes, I would do it again.

J.W.

Like a number of cars entered, the AC 16/80 of David Hescroff and Nigel Phillips was in concours condition — great to see cars like this really being used.

Lotus Cortinas and Minis were the favourites for overall best time; this 'Pre-65' classic saloon racing Ford was conducted by Alan McKay Firth and David Hunter into 10th place.

The Renault 8 Gordini of Dave Wheeler/John Evans sets off from the Castle Hotel ahead of our Rapier; an extremely rapid device, the Gordini finished only 7 secs down on the quickest Mini.

Proving the point that consistency and reliability count, this Morris 8 Series E with bowler-hatted crew (Derek Skinner and David Filsil) certainly didn't come last despite being very much the slowest car in the event.

CONTINUED FROM PAGE 31

repaired and the wheel arch stripped of old under sealant and painted with Jenoprimer.

The new panel slotted into place with a minimum of fuss, the major location being provided by the radius of the wheel arch, and next by the flanges in front panel and those adjacent to the bulkhead. As shown in the pictures, the rear six inches or so of the new panel were discarded and the join was made down the leading edge of the door pillar.

Being able to use these complete new panels (the other side is due to go on soon) has certainly advanced the rebuild considerably — fitting complete new major sections like this is almost invariably quicker than making up and fitting lots of small individual repair patches, something to be borne in mind during a rebuild if you are prevaricating about whether to buy a major new panel. It's usually well worth the outlay in terms of time and temper spared, and of course if you're paying someone to do the work this is doubly true.

However, as I mentioned at the outset we acknowledge that there can't be many of these particular panels floating around, so for the benefit of Rapier and Minx owners whose cars suffer from bad inner front wing rusting (and that must include most cars by now, such is the nature of this rust trap), in a later instalment we will be showing you how to form a repair section for this area, by means of templates and dimensions which we'll supply.

9

All mating surfaces were stripped of paint, oil and surface rust and the new panel finally clamped into place.

When the positioning was checked and rechecked, the spot welder was brought into play, the first welds being all round the wheel arch. Gas equipment was used where the panel met the door pillar as the spot welder's arms could not reach everywhere without fouling.

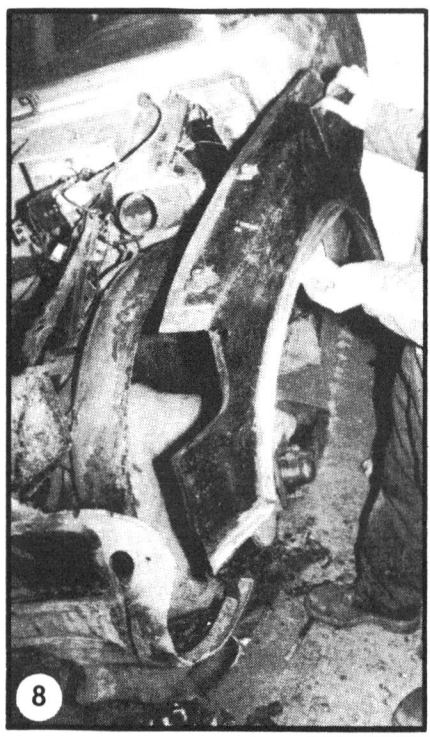

8

The new inner wing was offered up and final adjustments made to obtain a good fit.

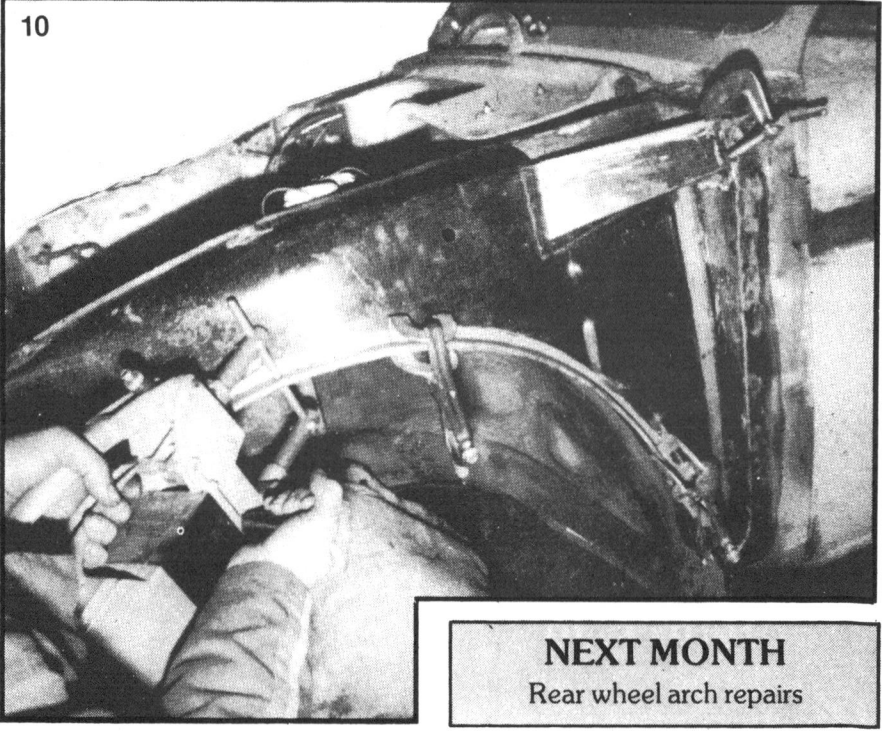

10

NEXT MONTH

Rear wheel arch repairs